797,885 Books

are available to read at

Forgotten Books

www.ForgottenBooks.com

Forgotten Books' App
Available for mobile, tablet & eReader

ISBN 978-1-333-42225-7
PIBN 10502446

This book is a reproduction of an important historical work. Forgotten Books uses state-of-the-art technology to digitally reconstruct the work, preserving the original format whilst repairing imperfections present in the aged copy. In rare cases, an imperfection in the original, such as a blemish or missing page, may be replicated in our edition. We do, however, repair the vast majority of imperfections successfully; any imperfections that remain are intentionally left to preserve the state of such historical works.

Forgotten Books is a registered trademark of FB &c Ltd.
Copyright © 2017 FB &c Ltd.
FB &c Ltd, Dalton House, 60 Windsor Avenue, London, SW19 2RR.
Company number 08720141. Registered in England and Wales.

For support please visit www.forgottenbooks.com

1 MONTH OF FREE READING

at
www.ForgottenBooks.com

By purchasing this book you are eligible for one month membership to ForgottenBooks.com, giving you unlimited access to our entire collection of over 700,000 titles via our web site and mobile apps.

To claim your free month visit: www.forgottenbooks.com/free502446

* Offer is valid for 45 days from date of purchase. Terms and conditions apply.

English
Français
Deutsche
Italiano
Español
Português

www.forgottenbooks.com

Mythology Photography **Fiction** Fishing Christianity **Art** Cooking Essays Buddhism Freemasonry Medicine **Biology** Music **Ancient Egypt** Evolution Carpentry Physics Dance Geology **Mathematics** Fitness Shakespeare **Folklore** Yoga Marketing **Confidence** Immortality Biographies Poetry **Psychology** Witchcraft Electronics Chemistry History **Law** Accounting **Philosophy** Anthropology Alchemy Drama Quantum Mechanics Atheism Sexual Health **Ancient History Entrepreneurship** Languages Sport Paleontology Needlework Islam **Metaphysics** Investment Archaeology Parenting Statistics Criminology **Motivational**

SEPTENARY MAN:

OR,

The Microcosm of the Macrocosm.

A STUDY OF THE HUMAN SOUL

In Relation to the Various Vehicles, or Avenues, of Consciousness, (Technically Known as the Seven Principles) by Means of which it Brings Itself into Relation with the Outer Cosmos; Including a Brief Examination of Dream and the Problems of Heredity.

BY

JEROME A. ANDERSON, M. D., F. T. S.

The Universe is composed of "the Same" and "the Other." PLATO.

THE LOTUS PUBLISHING COMPANY,
1170 Market Street, San Francisco, Cal.
The Path Office, 144 Madison Avenue, New York City.

December 25, 1895.

COPYRIGHT, 1895,
BY JEROME A. ANDERSON,
1170 Market Street,
SAN FRANCISCO, CALIFORNIA.

Dedicated to

H.

P.   B.

BY A GRATEFUL STUDENT.

PREFACE.

IN ISSUING this brief examination of the septenary classification of man's nature, the writer especially disclaims any authority for any statements contained therein other than as these appear reasonable, and as they seem to fit into and fill out vacant places in the theosophic philosophy. It is simply the work of an humble student, issued with the hope that it may assist fellow students.

The subject has been treated from the same standpoint as the writer's book upon Reincarnation. That is, the seven Principles of man have been studied from their scientific aspect solely. No proofs have been advanced except those capable of scientific demonstration. This scientific demonstration, of course, recognizes that logic, philosophy, and reason afford the very highest proof of which any metaphysical problem is capable. It has also been held that, where other more direct proofs seemed wanting, analogy might be applied without warranting any charge of dogmatic assertion, and that the laws governing matter and force, and the aspects of consciousness, upon one plane of the Cosmos might be reasonably carried over into other planes. Therefore, when dealing with such abstruse metaphysical problems as Atma, Buddhi, or Prana, for example, the proofs of their existence and nature must of necessity lie largely along philosophical and logical lines, while the more material Principles, as the Linga Sharira, together with some aspects of Kama and Manas, have been studied, and their nature deduced from their observed behavior upon this, the molecular, plane of the Universe.

The writer makes no claim to that intuitional perception which grasps truth without the necessity of logical analysis. He can only grope along the paths of analogy and reason. Therefore, while admitting the work of intuitional writers to be much more valuable, he still believes there is a large class of his fellow students who, like himself, must perforce adopt the lower method, and to such it is hoped the book will appeal; and also that it may be of some service to the great cause we all serve—Humanity.

J. A. A.

CONTENTS.

INTRODUCTION.

MAN, THE MICROCOSM.—An Old Teaching—Nature of the Macrocosm—Spirit and Matter—Vehicles of the One Consciousness—Seven Great Divisions—Dominant Vibration Constitutes a "Round"—Soul Specially Related to a Particular Hierarchy during a Round, Nature of Incarnation, etc.. 9

CHAPTER I.

THE BODY.—All "Bodies" must Correspond to the "Matter" of any particular Round—The Pathway to Form and Incarnation—Senses not in the Physical Body, Proofs—Cycles Governing Incarnation—Latent Force, What—Hierarchies of Builders—Compound Source of Bodily Entities, etc.. 27

CHAPTER II.

THE LINGA SHARIRA.—Composed of Third Round Matter—Plastic under Thought—Theory of Emanations—Source of Linga Sharira, its Functions and Fate—Cause of all Form—Preserver of Species—"Seance Phenomena," etc.. 40

CHAPTER III.

PRANA.—Universal Principle—Manifested Jiva—Relation to the Soul and Body—"Fiery Lives"—Monads—Cycles of Life, etc................. 52

CHAPTER IV.

KAMA.—Consciousness in the State of Desire—Source of—Nature of—Relation to Thought—Individualizing Effect of Kama—Animal Desire—Relation of Instinct to Desire and to Intuition—A Human Elemental Synthesizes the Body—Nature of this Elemental—A Glimpse of Man's Microcosm—The Effect of Death—Reincarnation of the Personality, How, Why—Effect of Suicide, Accident, etc................ 63

CHAPTER V.

LOWER MANAS.—The True Soul Seeking to Express Itself in Molecular Matter—The Two Forces in each Human Breast—The Nature of Incarnation—Magnetism Imparted to Non-Magnetic Iron—The Conserver of One Life's Experiences—Cycle of Conscious Life Terminates with Devachan—Conflict of Manas with Kama—Loss of the Soul, etc....... 74

CONTENTS.

CHAPTER VI.

HIGHER MANAS.—The Thinking Principle—Nature of—Powers of—Immortality of—Compassionate Mission of—Divine Potencies and Potentialities—"Mind Born Sons"—Emanation or Fission a Process of Generation upon all Planes of Nature, etc............................ 84

CHAPTER VII.

THE HIGHER TRIAD—ATMA, BUDDHI, AND MANAS.—Metaphysical Difficulties in their Conception—Nature of Atma—"The Emanating Spark of the Uncreated Ray"—Nature of Buddhi—Store House of Cosmic Wisdom—Giver of True Immortality, etc............................. 95

CHAPTER VIII.

THE DREAMING SELF.—Nature and Importance of Dream—Key to Inner Conditions afforded by—An Entity Who Dreams Each Dream, etc...... 104

CHAPTER IX.

THE PROBLEMS OF HEREDITY.—Absurdity of Materialistic Hypotheses—The Differing Streams of Heredity—Physical, Mental, and Spiritual—All Inheritance Proceeds Under the Law of Cause and Effect—Relation of the Unit, Man, to Humanity as a Whole, or Racial, National, and Family Heredity—Man the Arbiter of his Own Destiny, etc........ 114

INTRODUCTION.

MAN, THE MICROCOSM.

IN THE days when religion, science, and philosophy were but differing aspects of Theosophy, or "God-Wisdom," all united in recognizing in man a compound, or complex, nature. Thus, Brahmanism, or more correctly, the Vedantin schools of Brahmanism, held, and still holds, that he has at least four or five Principles, or vehicles of consciousness, entering into his composition. Buddhism recognizes seven; Confucianism, five; Gnosticism, seven; the Kabala, seven; and Christianity, three. The same teaching can be very clearly verified in the old Egyptian symbology, and in the earlier as well as the later Greek philosophy, particularly in Neo-Platonism. While testimony can never have the weight of evidence, still, where it assumes the universal character which this teaching has had in all ages of the world's history, it really ceases to be merely testimony, and approximates very closely to the standard of evidence. That man, because of his complex yet divine nature, is the Microcosm of the Macrocosm, or Cosmos, has been a semi-esoteric teaching for ages. It was implied in the old Grecian exhortation, "Man, Know Thyself," meaning that within his own being was to be found the key to the mysteries of the universe about him. Later, the same half-veiled truth appears in the Hermetic and Rosicrucian maxim, "As above, so below." It is now, and perhaps for the first time for ages, made entirely exoteric, and explained to the whole world as one of the chief of the philosophical concepts of Theosophy, under the popu-

INTRODUCTION.

lar as well as technical term, "The Seven Principles of Man."*

It must not be understood that man is now actually the Microcosm of the Macrocosm. He is only potentially so. Within his being reside, *in potentia*, all the potencies in the manifested universe about him; but not *in actu*, except as he shall, by his own will, realize them. The importance, therefore, of the recognition of this awe-inspiring fact becomes at once apparent, as well as the potent factor the knowledge of it must prove in stimulating spiritual development.

If man be, then, the Microcosm of the Macrocosm, what is the nature of that Macrocosm? for the assertion of a comparison implies and, indeed, necessitates at least partial sameness or equality, else there can be nothing to compare. Without attempting to answer that which is unanswerable, or to deal with the Unknowable Source from which all finite being must have emanated, the teaching of the Wisdom Religion in regard to this is, that all the infinite diversity of the manifested universe arose out of, or rather within, Absolute Unity, which thus assumes the relation to the cosmos of a Causeless Cause—a Cause which, while it is of necessity the basis of all manifested life, remains itself ever unmanifested; untouched in its absolute essence by all the great differentiation which arises within it, and which constitutes the finite universe. At the primal appearance of finite manifestation, there appear two great aspects of this Absolute Unity, termed respectively Spirit and Matter; these two being in reality but opposite poles, or modes of expression, of the One Unity. Thus, behind all manifestation lies the ever-concealed Causeless Cause;

---

*These seven Principles will be fully discussed as we proceed, but for present use they may be enumerated as:

SANSCRIT TERMS.	ENGLISH EQUIVALENTS (APPROXIMATELY).
Sthula Sharira	The Body.
Linga Sharira	Astral Body.
Prana	Vitality.
Kama	Animal Soul (Desire).
Manas	Human Soul (Thought).
Budhi	Spiritual Soul (Intuition).
Atma or Jiva	Spirit.

and all that which we perceive and conceive as the manifested universe is simply the illusory—because the finite cannot measure nor comprehend the infinite—aspects of this Causeless Cause, projected in time and space like shadows from a magic-lantern, and quite as unreal in that they are not themselves the real things which they thus seem. But even shadows must have something real to cause them, so that though the manifested universe, owing to our finite capacities, must remain for us a shadow and a type, it rests of necessity upon a real basis of Infinite Being.

Of these two Primal Aspects, then, one appears to us as spirit, or consciousness; the other, as matter; and once the two pass into finite manifestation their action and reaction reveal a third great absolute aspect, which appears as motion, or force. It is further taught that spirit and matter mutually limit each other—that spirit, or one pole of this manifestation of the Causeless Cause, becomes knowable to us by means of the limitations of matter; while, on the other hand, matter also becomes knowable, or manifested to us, by means of the action of spirit; the two being, as we have seen, but aspects of the same Unknowable Unity; that which appears to us as matter including in its essence spirit; that which seems to us spirit including in its essence matter.

The universe, then, may be said to be composed of matter and of spirit, each causing the other to manifest in an infinite diversity, and which manifested diversity constitutes the Macrocosm. This, therefore, consists from its conscious aspect of infinite states of consciousness; the entire universe thus being but embodied, or matter-limited, consciousness. In other words, the spiritual or conscious-aspect of nature, being limited by the material aspect, causes the appearance of form; while form, assuming intelligent adaptations to environment, betrays the indwelling spirit or consciousness. The expression of higher, more perfect, and less material forms, would seem to constitute the process of evolution, as the consequent widening of the conscious area through such experiences, until infinite consciousness is again reached, would appear to be its motive.

It is evident, also, that a study of man as the Microcosm of the great Macrocosm involves and implies the recognition within him, and the examination, of all states of consciousness, from those which are classed as the most grossly material to those of the highest conceivable spirituality. A careful analysis, however, reduces these infinite potencies and potentialities to seven great divisions, which in man are classed as Principles, and, in the cosmos as Hierarchies. From the standpoint of consciousness, these Principles become merely more or less material vehicles of consciousness for its limiting to one or other of the great hierarchical cosmic planes. For it cannot be too strongly iterated that matter limits consciousness always, and that, for this reason, though a Principle be a vehicle as regards a particular plane or Hierarchy of cosmos, it is a hindrance or obstacle in regard to all other states or planes. A human Principle must, therefore, be regarded as limiting the human consciousness to a particular plane, just as the human soul must be looked upon as a (potential) center of infinite consciousness, limited by material vehicles which it is striving to overcome, one by one, as it journeys through its evolutionary Cycle of Necessity back to its Source.

It seems necessary, then, in dealing with these vehicles of consciousness in man, to approach their study from their material aspect, because Principles, or states of consciousness, seem most conceivable, or at least most easily explained, when looked at through their limiting vehicles. By this method, too, if unable to explain them, we at least state the problems involved in finite terms.

The teaching is, then, that consciousness throughout the universe may be divided into seven great states; a teaching which even modern material science corroborates in its recognition of matter in seven differing conditions. These conditions or states represent: 1, the homogeneous; 2, the "radiant" matter of Professor Crookes; 3, curd-like or nebulous matter, as manifested in the nebulæ in the heavens; 4, "atomic" matter, or the beginning of differentiation; 5, the germinal or fiery state, in which the differing elements we now recognize under the aspects of air, water, fire, and earth are beginning to assume their future properties; 6, astral, or ethereal matter; and, 7, earthy, molecular matter, or the present condition of the matter of this planet in its cold, dead aspect of dependency upon the sun for life and vitality.

Recognizing that all forms of matter are caused by and associated with corresponding states of consciousness, if these forms of matter thus associated with our solar system be related to its states of consciousness, the following correspondences are at least permissible—premising that the correspondence only indicates the action of a certain Hierarchy of cosmic consciousness as limited by the material conditions of our own solar system, and not* that this approaches the state of the same consciousness not so inhibited, or limited. [Matter in its homogeneous condition corresponds to Jiva, or Atma,* or Unmanifested life—a state too near the infinite to be comprehensible by finite beings. The "radiant" state of matter may be compared to Buddhic† consciousness, or pure consciousness, which *knows* without reasoning. Nebulous matter, again, is related to Mahatic‡ consciousness, or that of thought. In the matter of the nebulæ is the prophesy and potency of the future worlds and their varied conscious beings, of which the nebulæ are thus the Mahatic, or prophetic, thought. Atomic, or differentiated, matter corresponds to the Fohatic state of consciousness, for Fohat§ is essentially "desire," and desire for union in this atomic state results in the molecular aggregations which make physical forms possible. Again, the germinal, or fiery, condition of matter corresponds to Prana, or manifested Life, as contrasted with the unmanifested, unknowable, or Jivic, aspect of Life. Astral matter corresponds to all the mysterious

---
*The universal source of the Jiva, or Atman, of man's seventh Principle.
†Buddhi—the hierarchal source of the sixth human Principle.
‡Mahat—"the Great One." Hierarchal source of man's Thinking Principle—Manas. The "Over-Soul" (in one aspect).
§Fohat—cosmic electricity, or "nerve fluid," (in one aspect). The universal source of the fourth Principle in man, Kama, or desire. Cosmic will-desire.

states of reflected consciousness, of which the phenomena of hypnotism, trance, clairvoyance, etc., are illustrations. All such are examples of consciousness not normal to any given plane, but reflected from above or below. Earthy, or molecular, matter corresponds to physical, or sense, consciousness, or that of time, space, and form, as they arise in consciousness through the physical senses.

Thus, by means of these correspondences may be obtained a glimpse, or faint idea, of the seven great hierarchal states of consciousness, out of which arise man's seven Principles, or those states of consciousness in the Microcosm which correspond to the Seven Hierarchies in the Macrocosm. All differing conditions of matter appear to arise through differing rates of vibration, and Prof. Crookes, in his "Genesis of the Elements," has pictured a way in which it is possible, through changes of vibration, for matter to assume infinitely differing properties, and thus become a vehicle for infinitely differing states of consciousness. To illustrate:

Let us suppose a nebulous mass, or fire-mist, occupying an immense area in space, and having a certain definite vibration. The slightest change in this vibration would cause matter to appear, within the original fire-mist matter, with entirely new properties, and bring the whole mass more definitely under the action of "gravitation" (molecular attraction, wrongly termed "molar" by scientists). Tending towards a common "laya," or neutral center, it would constantly assume differing qualities, and take on differing and continually lower vibrations, through all the stages of a condensing, by an apparently mechanical process, into a world. And as each downward change involves an increasing limitation of consciousness, it is easy to see how increasingly "material" human, as well as a nature, Principles arise. It is also easy to see that the whole process may be a deliberate and voluntary descent, or changing of spiritual into material conditions, by beings seeking widening consciousness through passing from pole to pole of the spiritual and material aspects of the Absolute—these being the necessary horizons of all finite Intelligences, however high or holy. This descent would represent the involution arc of the great cycle of Being, while the ascent out of material conditions would constitute that which modern science partially recognizes in its incomplete theory of evolution.

But, aside from metaphysical generalizations, Prof. Crookes has shown the important part which simple changes of vibration in the same substance must play; and he has constructed a most ingenious diagram to illustrate the action of time, space, and temperature in producing new "elements" by these agents, through the modifications of the old. The point of interest in relation to the septenary cosmos and Microcosm is that he supposes a series of fourteen elements to have been produced by cycles of electrical currents, thus exactly duplicating the Brahmanical fourteen Lokas, or two aspects (divine and terrestrial) of each of the seven Hierarchies. He then makes among these groupings seven "dominant atomicities," again unconsciously following Occultism in his methods. His diagram of a lemniscate figure also shows how much the ancients knew in regard to those things of which we conceive them to have been so ignorant, for it is almost a replica of one of the oldest symbols known—the Greek Caduceus. This consists of two serpents twined about a common staff, crossing each other in the manner of a lemniscate. He supposes a series of differing elements, arising through the pressure of matter in a centripetal direction in the condensation of the original fire-mist, and from these at differing cycles of that condensation would be produced a new series of elements. That is to say, that the ripple of vibration in the fire-mist form of matter would, as it tends centripetally during a certain cycle, produce a certain series of elements. Another electrical cycle, temperature having changed, would produce a series of elements nearly, but not exactly, like the first.

In his illustration Prof. Crookes shows that, supposing the first great cycle to have produced fourteen elements, then, in repeating that cycle with a lower temperature, at each point at which an original element was generated one corresponding in all its original attributes would be produced. Thus, the first fourteen elements being lithium, beryllium, boron, carbon, nitrogen, oxygen, fluorine, sodium, magnesium, aluminum, silicon, phosphorus, sulphur and chlorine, the first of the second cycle would be potassium, which is the "lineal descendant" of lithium, and so on, down through a series which comprises seven of these "lineal descendants," for each of the original fourteen elements.

From the mechanical aspect of manifestation, the universe is produced solely by modifications in the eternal motion resulting from the action of spirit upon matter—a theory which, in the East, is beautifully and poetically symbolized in the "Great Breath" of Vedantin philosophy. These modifications are orderly, as they must needs be in a law-governed cosmos, and, while covering vast and unrealizable abysses of time, have yet been made the subject of mathematical speculation.

The time in which a key-note or dominant mode of vibration maintains itself throughout a planetary mass is denominated, in theosophical nomenclature, a "Round." During this period the "matter" of the planet, even to the most ethereal of its seven "Globes,"* or planes of matter and states of consciousness, assumes characteristics determined by the dominant vibration; and while it persists the Ego, or soul, has to undergo and assimilate all experiences possible under these conditions. Then the dominant vibration will change, new forms of matter and new material experiences being thus provided to permit of an ever widening of the conscious area of the Ego, passing through its complete cycle of evolution. In the downward arc, or involution into material

---

*The earth has likewise its seven Principles, corresponding to those of man. The states of matter, force, and consciousness which collectively form each of these Principles is technically termed a "globe," while a "round" is the time required for the soul to pass through each of the entire seven. For a full explanation of "globes" and "rounds," see the Secret Doctrine, and other theosophical works.

states, each successive cycle of vibration becomes more material—that is to say, the substance-aspect of the Unknowable preponderates more and more in proportion. But a limit must eventually be reached, because this is a finite process, and Theosophy teaches that this limit has been reached in the present Fourth, or molecular, Round of this earth, and that when the next hour shall strike, and the dominant vibration change, entities upon the earth will retrace the process of their involution into matter, and regain their former astral consciousness, with self-consciousness added thereto. Indeed, this process is already under way, and even the earth itself has been becoming less "material" since the midway point of this Round was reached some millions of years since.

This earth, therefore, is now in a condition of molecular vibration, and in its fourth, or kamic, or desire, Round, which Round will last so long as the "life" wave or impulse has its activity in molecular matter; for the monadic or Dhyan-Chohanic impulse which constitutes this life-wave passes from globe to globe, arousing each to activity and leaving it comparatively dead, or in its "pralaya," much as a circling rainstorm might pass from point to point over a sea, arousing and churning into a furious but transient activity each successive portion over which it passes, and leaving it comparatively *in statu quo* until it returns. But the duration of each dominant mode of vibration covers an immense cycle of time, and, in Brahmanical literature, is called a Day of Brahmâ, and is a period involving some 4,320 millions of years. This is the astronomical period required for all the planets of our system to be in conjunction; an event which may well produce even physical causes sufficient to terminate or entirely change the condition of physical existence on one or more planets. This cycle will comprise the duration of this world in its present state, before it goes into pralaya, or changes the present for another rate of vibration, which will constitute another Round.

The Theosophic classification of men into seven great Races

during each of the seven Rounds, or differing material states of the earth, is another recognition of the fact that, in our present universe, the number seven is the dominant one for its entire duration. It must not be understood that during any particular Round only one mode of vibration is present. At least those of each of the Seven creative Hierarchies are all in activity, for these constitute or cause the (in Theosophical teachings) seven companion "globes" of each planet, of which our earth and all earths visible to us is the Fourth. These, by their combinations and correlations, produce the "forty-nine fires" of Eastern occultism. But one of these Hierarchies is dominant during any particular Round, and to appreciate or reach to the consciousness of the others requires special and, in a sense, abnormal development. Yet, during certain portions of each Round each of the seven human Principles is brought into special relations with the dominant vibration, or mode of consciousness, and from this arises the characteristics which distinguish and constitute each Race.

To illustrate: Our world is, as stated, in the fourth Round, and the fourth, a kamic, Hierarchy is dominant throughout its entire duration. But it is also in its fifth subdivision of that Round, and therefore, under the cyclic law, is specially related to the fifth, or manasic, Principle, which thus becomes subdominant, or the chief undertone during the race cycle. For this reason we appear to have intellectuality dominant, but it is only in appearance. In reality desire—the characteristic of the entire fourth Round—is utilizing mind to increase the pleasures of sensuous perception in the great mass of the race, and mankind is, therefore, said to be in the kama-manasic state. Now, in the next Round, the vibration of thought, or manas, will be dominant throughout the Round; but when we get to the fourth division of that great cycle and enter its fourth Race the present relation of desire and thought will be reversed, and we shall be in a condition of manas-kamic instead of kama-manasic, as at present. Manas, or thought, will be the ruling Principle, and Kama will be a subtone, and be in a similar condition of servitude to thought that thought now sustains towards desire. At present desire is master of thought. Then thought will be the master of desire. And similarly for all the Rounds. Each of the seven Principles will be specially and regularly related to the consciousness of the Ego because of these subdominant cycles of each Creative Hierarchy included in the great cycle, Round, or Day of Brahma, and in this manner constitute the seven natural divisions termed Races.

But how are man's Principles directly derived? That is to say, what is the immediate relation between the human Principles and the great cosmic Hierarchies? All cosmic Principles are divine and pure, of necessity. That which we term desire, and which we are taught to "kill out," is, in its essence, a purely divine state of consciousness. An attempt at an explanation is this:

A human soul is a center of consciousness, arising we know not how. It roots in the Unknowable. It passes through all of the lower kingdoms of nature, widening its consciousness all the while, until, in unthinkable periods of time, it at last reaches a condition of self-consciousness, or a state in which it recognizes that it is conscious, and examines and reasons upon its own conscious states. We might trace an evolutionary pathway, which would have at least the warrant of analogy, thus:* A center of consciousness differentiating within the Absolute unites itself with pure primordial matter, acquires the experiences of this association, which might be distinguished as atomic, and passes onward to enter molecular matter, in which state it synthesizes two or more atoms, already the seat of a more primal form of consciousness, into form as its new body. And so on, step by step, until at length it reaches the self-conscious state, and synthesizes for itself a body already occupied by hosts of lower entities. The consciousness of these lower entities, in man's body as well as in

---

*For a fuller statement of this hypothesis see Author's work, "Reincarnation," chapter on "Individualization of the Soul."

nature, is derived from high creative beings, termed, in the East, Dhyan Chohans. These great and divine entities clothe themselves in lower states of matter in a manner analogous to that by which the human Ego incarnates in its body, and impart to this matter their consciousness, and give to it that impulse which takes it up through all the lower evolutionary steps. And the added consciousness which the entities ensouling this matter thus obtain by emanation from these High Beings is pure and unmarred by reason—an instance of which is seen in that consciousness by means of which chemical atoms seek unerringly their affinities. Similarly, the center of consciousness of man, in its evolutionary course upward, arrives at a state where it clothes itself with "matter" ensouled by entities having this lower yet divine consciousness. Thus, in this Round man is clothed almost entirely by entities whose normal consciousness is pure desire. This consciousness is divine and natural; it is a step in that divine sequence which constitutes evolution. The human Ego, incarnating here for the purpose of gaining experience, is brought into relation with these desire-entities that it may experience this consciousness. But the human Ego, being inexperienced and ignorant, allows its own divine, reasoning nature to be swayed by that desire which, while perfectly normal in these entities which constitute its body, is abnormal and unnatural for itself. By incarnating in these desire-swayed animal bodies, the Ego thus obtains the opportunity to view the play of passion, from its divine and reasoning attitude. But the part of spectator does not satisfy. So close is the union produced by incarnation that the ray of Manas which intellectualizes the human-animal brain falls under the illusion that itself and its body are identical, and rages and fights with all the fury of one whom the struggle concerns. This illusion is caused by the dominance of the kamic Principle during the fourth Round. But the fifth, or manasic subcycle of this Round being now in progress, that Principle is being immensely strengthened by the influx from its Hierarchy; so that, as this is the turning or lowest point of the evolutionary arc, the fight for supremacy between Thought and Desire is taking place now, and for many human souls is being settled for this Manvantara, or man-completing cycle.

The relation of Principle to Hierarchy, then, is that of attribute to its source; and, in the case of the Manasic Hierarchy, of parent to child. Each of the seven states of consciousness which constitute man's Principles is derived from a different Hierarchy, or Host; the lower Principles coming from the diffused Dhyan Chohanic impulse upon matter. When this impulse has pushed the evolutionary process sufficiently high, then other and higher entities incarnate in man, and bestow upon him his Thinking Principle, thus lifting his consciousness to a higher plane.

In this manner, then, is man shown to be the Microcosm of the Macrocosm. If we find in him these Principles of Desire, or Thought, or, still higher, of Divine Intuition, we must postulate and accept a source for them. Theosophy does not assume creation out of nothing. The presence in man of the ability to think, the force of desire, the power of intuition, or any of the things which make up his being, necessitates postulating a source for each. It is, also, unphilosophic to suppose that a stream can rise higher than its source, to use a physical illustration. Therefore, so far from accepting, with materialism, that consciousness is the result of molecular vibration, Theosophy postulates as the source of man's conscious Principles divine Principles almost infinitely higher than their lesser reflections in him. Every effect must have its cause. The power to think must have origin somewhere. Shall we accept the absurdity of something arising out of nothing? or the theosophical teaching that these Principles are derived from great cosmic or hierarchal states of consciousness? The latter must appeal to any reasoning being.

A further proof that man is the Microcosm of the Macrocosm is found in the fact that in his physical body he synthesizes all the known forces in nature. All systems of levers, all possible physical motion, is there exemplified. All states of consciousness in nature are also in his body. The consciousness which is in the stone is found in his bones; that of vegetable life, in the hairs of his head; the consciousness of all stages of animal life is found in the differing cells and organs of his body; so that man is the Microcosm of all nature about us of which we can conceive. It is, therefore, reasonable to suppose that he is likewise the Microcosm of the inconceivable side of nature.

Man's Seven Principles, then, are: The Body, which limits his consciousness to perceptions of form, time, and space by means of the senses. Prana, which gives rise to, and is the consciousness of, life. The Linga Sharira, which relates him to astral or reflected consciousness. Kama, which relates him to the consciousness of desire. Manas, which relates him to consciousness of consciousness, or self-consciousness. Buddhi, which relates him to intuitional consciousness; consciousness above thought—in which no thought is necessary. And, finally, Atma, wherein all consciousness, and all states of consciousness, are synthesized.

We will err, however, in our further study if we consider man as the product of evolution, as this term is commonly understood. There is no evolution, in the scientific use of the word. There is a great becoming, which, as already partially explained, proceeds somewhat in this manner: There streams out from the Absolute the Seven great Rays, Breaths, or Hierarchies, of creative being, before referred to. Without pausing to analyze their combinations and differentiations, let us suppose that each of these great Hierarchies ensouls a portion of cosmic Substance. Within the limits of each Hierarchy, an evolution is possible from a lower to a more intense degree of the particular consciousness of the Hierarchy. But for a being ensouled by, let us say, kamic to reach the manasic or thought consciousness by evolving up to and into it out of the kamic, is as impossible as it is absurd. Not all the forces of the kamic plane can produce one single rational thought. There must come entities, having the power of thought, and bestow this power by emanation, ere thought can be born. Therefore, it is idle to say that man evolves up and through the animal kingdom as man. As a Microcosm of the Macrocosm, as a potential center of consciousness upon every plane of the Cosmos by virtue of his being sprung from and a portion of the Absolute itself, the center of consciousness in man has experienced all these states; but it was not as man while so doing. Not until he was touched by the flame of thought did man become a thinker and a man.

When, therefore, a center of consciousness is in a certain "kingdom" it is helpless to win its way up and out of that kingdom. For it, "evolution" is a meaningless word. If it be locked in the stony embrace of the mineral kingdom, there it must remain until help from above enables it to pass out of this state. If it be a vegetable or an animal, it is equally helpless. Caught in that part of the cycle of necessity where Kama* holds sway, it can only experience and make kamic feeling its own. But when it reaches the very fulness of this, it has also reached a point where thought is able to weld or fuse itself to the kamically heated mass, and a thinking soul is born.

As a pilgrim through all these hierarchies of consciousness, man may be said to evolve; but the cause of his evolution is an emanation from above, not a pushing up from below. And the true man really never was an animal, nor a lower being of any sort. Birth, as man, occurs when that Hierarchy is reached and its emanation becomes possible; but did not self-conscious beings descend or incarnate in the animal bodies not all the evolutionary forces acting throughout all the eternities could produce a man. Life may be received from one Hierarchy, form from another, and desire may be born from the emanation of a third; but the entity is still not a man until Manas, or Thought, stoops and claims him for its own.

And this is not the work of an instant, as we mark time, but

---

*Kama—Desire, uninfluenced by thought or reason.

occupies untold ages in its birth-throes. For Thought must reach down and lay hold of the purely kamic entity, and struggle sore and long ere the new being is sure of his foothold among the gods.

This, then, constitutes man the Microcosm of the Macrocosm: that he holds within his being all potentialities of that Macrocosm, and that he has received from the great Creative Hierarchies their creative emanations, and, with the impress of Manas, or Thought, upon his brow, is winning his way back toward the Source from whence he came, *plus* the self-consciousness bestowed by Thought. Equally with man, however, may every atom in the Universe be said to be the Microcosm, for each holds all the potentialities of the Great Whole. Man is but the pure, virgin gold, passing through the hand of many hierarchies of workmen, and receiving the impress of each. But each can bestow but its own nature, and so man is not man until he reaches a point where Mind-Dhyanas take him in hand, and bestow their last, best, yet oft-times fatal gift. In the ebbing and flowing of consciousness within the seas of lower hierarchies the centers of consciousness may fuse and blend, flow upward and recede, for all is below the plane of self-conscious thought. Only at the very farthest borders of Kama has the ripple of differentiation reached that degree at which it becomes possible for a new and distinct entity to be born. Below this, the rising and falling of conscious life can scarcely be called evolution, nor can the entities so engaged be said to be either advancing or retrograding.

All entities in Nature, then, are in the throes of a great becoming, which might be called evolution, if the proper methods by which this becoming is accomplished were understood. Within each Hierarchy there is an ebbing and flowing of consciousness, and this process may be said to be evolution, in, perhaps, the scientific sense of the term. But from Hierarchy to Hierarchy no evolution is possible. The lifting is done by the direct bestowing of the essence of the higher upon the lower entity. This great fact must be kept distinctly in mind in all the study of Man and his Principles which will be had in this volume. By it can be understood the relation of the true Thinking Man to his lower reflection. By it may be seen how, and why, and where, the struggle of Mind with Passion takes place, and a ray of philosophical light thus thrown across the darkly-passionate pages of human existence.

SEPTENARY MAN

OR

THE MICROCOSM OF THE MACROCOSM.

CHAPTER I.

THE BODY.

THE BODY, or the tabernacle of the clay in which man's soul dwells, is the first or the seventh, accordingly as numbered, of the seven Principles or aspects of consciousness into which Theosophy divides the human constitution. Its office is to relate man's center of consciousness or soul to matter in a condition of molecular activity, or to that rate of vibration which constitutes the fourth Round. Upon this earth, or Globe " D " of theosophic nomenclature, this molecular Round represents the very apotheosis of impermanency of states of consciousness as well as of form. During its cycle, change follows upon change with an almost infinite rapidity; integration and disintegration succeed each other with the swiftness of thought, and effect treads upon the heels of cause with a celerity impossible upon higher planes of being and in more stable states of matter. Consequently, the soul has here its greatest opportunities for setting up causes, either good or evil, and for quickly experiencing their effects, and hence of rapidly acquiring knowledge and wisdom. Therefore, this molecular plane has been rightly termed the great schoolhouse of the soul.

As we shall see in the proper connection, the true soul of man is out of all harmonic relation with molecular consciousness. In order, then, that it may reach this, it becomes necessary for it to approach it by utilizing specially prepared molecular avenues. It therefore constructs for itself a body composed of molecules capable of receiving the impressions caused by the contact of other molecules and the molecular forces having here their normal field of activity, and in this manner assimilates molecular consciousness. This is the sole office of the body as such—to bring the soul within the area of molecular activities; to cause it to become sensitive to, or conscious of, molecular vibrations. It is not the seat of sensation—understanding by sensation the impressions that the soul receives from the senses, or the experience it gets through hearing, seeing, smelling, tasting, and touching or contact. None of these are located in the physical body, but in an inner or astral one, which will be the subject of the next chapter.

That the senses are not seated in the body, is capable of demonstration in many ways, chief among which are the phenomena of hypnotism. In this state it is possible for the will of the hypnotizer to interpose between the subject and his senses, and to inhibit the hearing, seeing, tasting, feeling, or smelling of the latter at will. Thus one, yielding to the hypnotic trance, can be made to taste water as vinegar, vinegar as water, quinine as sugar, and *vice versa;* or, in the case of sight, made to see, or prevented from seeing, anything the hypnotizer wills. For example: If forbidden to see a certain person while permitted to see his hat, the result is that the hat is seen floating about in the air, while the subject is quite unconscious of the fact that there is a man wearing it. If the senses were in the body this phenomenon would be impossible, for after the impact of the vibrations of light they would be transferred along the molecules of the optic nerve and impinge upon and set up motion in the molecules of the physical brain, and the will of another—or even of one's self—could not prevent, once it formed upon the retina, the picture of the complete man, hat and all, being transmitted to the brain and there recorded as a conscious experience, if the senses really were in the physical molecules of the brain. A physical sequence of a physical eye, a physical optic nerve, and physical molecules of the brain, cannot be interrupted except by physical means. Therefore, when an outside will interposes between the power of sight, hearing, or either of the senses, and their objects, it is evident that the centers of sensation are not in the molecules of man's physical brain, but must lie more deeply within his being. It will be seen, also, that herein is one of the proofs of the existence of the soul.

The human body, then, is built up of countless hosts of molecules synthesized into cells by units of consciousness having their normal existence upon the molecular plane. These latter derive their energy and vitality from those which the "Secret Doctrine" terms "fiery lives"—that is to say, from the almost homogeneous, electrical "world stuff" which represents the dawn of cosmic differentiation, and whose center of energy is the sun. The infinitely active energies of these fiery lives, radiating as that which we recognize as light, heat, electricity, vital force, etc., are intercepted and directed or synthesized in order to construct molecular bodies by units of consciousness descending to the molecular plane. The action is similar to that of the millwright who takes advantage of the flowing stream of water to direct it through his turbine wheels to move his machinery. Or it may be, rather, more like the action of the farmer who takes advantage of the generative forces of springtime to sow the seed for his future crops. Force so intercepted and utilized becomes the so-called "latent" energies. All latent energy is but the restricting of the original fire-mist rate of vibration within molecular limits. In the mineral kingdom, this latency may persist for an entire globe-Round,* and in the vegetable kingdom, even, during those enormous periods represented in such examples as the giant sequoia of California, which botanists assert were living in the (supposed) days of Solomon. But in the animal and human-animal kingdoms the life cycles of entities are shorter; and, while the force of the downward cycle of a reëmbodying entity is sufficient to control into an orderly sequence the action of the fiery lives, yet, when that cycle begins to wane, the force relaxes, and, from being "builders," these now become "destroyers"; and their energies, no longer controlled by the "elemental"† which synthesizes the human body,

---

*Globe-Round—the duration of evolutionary activity upon any one of earth's seven globes. One-seventh of a Round.

†The lower entity which synthesizes the body viewed as a merely animal form. All animals have similar "elemental souls," or centers of consciousness. See later on.

are seized upon by the numberless parasites, or "microbes," which infest it, and utilized to finally break up the form which the same energies originally constructed. Except for this action, nature would be but one vast cemetery of "dead" forms, awaiting the termination of the Round.

The fact that man is the microcosm of the macrocosm is illustrated in the progressive steps of his reëmbodiment. These show that there are within his being, either actually or potentially, all states of consciousness, all modes of motion, and all the conditions of matter in the universe about him. As the pranic vibration of the fiery lives descends to successive planes, innumerable entities which have been associated with man in past lives awaken to renewed activity and life. It is the enforced attendance of these entities which constitutes man the microcosm of the macrocosm, and his cycles of objective and subjective life are their relative manvantaras* and pralayas. For, just as a world comes into being out of fire-mist, and descends through all the differing states of matter until it reaches its lowest point in the rocks, and then re-ascends the evolutionary cycle until it loses all form at the culmination of the spiritual portion of its arc, carrying in both its upward and downward sweep hosts of entities synthesized by its great Rector, so is the body of man formed by, and the incarnation of, associated entities, with whose evolution he is also especially connected as their chief, or Rector. As the energy of these fiery lives passes downward through ethereal and astral into molecular matter, at each plane the awakened entities clothe themselves with its "matter," until at length they reach the physical, and their reincarnation is accomplished. Chief of these, and synthesizer of each human body, is that which is known as a "human" elemental. The return of this elemental to incarnation necessitates and involves the construction of the outer, physical form in its entirety, as it is the chief Rector of the body as such, and stands in relation to the true man, or reincarnating ego, much as does the Rector of the earth to the Rectors of the "divine" planets. For, as the "Secret Doctrine" states, "The Lha which turns the

---

*Manvantara—a man-perfecting cycle or evolutionary period. Pralaya—an equal period of "rest," or subjective as opposed to objective existence.

Fourth is servant to the Lhas of the Seven." And although undoubtedly the next manvantaric step forward of the process of evolution will bring this entity upon the human plane, at present it is but a single step in advance of other and similar elementals which synthesize the bodies of the animals in the next kingdom below. Some of the higher of these would appear to be at present more fitted to step upward to the human-elemental plane than are those in human form fitted to pass on into completed human beings—so greatly have we failed in our duty of controlling and spiritualizing these our turbulent associates.

Thus, at each step in the process of reincarnating, the human soul is related successively to more and more material "bodies," until these culminate in the grossly physical encasement in which it dwells while in molecular environments. Nature eternally repeats her processes; and so man, in reincarnating, returns with the "matter," similar to that of Globe D of the first Round as his first "body"; for in each Round all bodies must correspond to and be composed of the "matter" of each particular globe of that Round. Thus his bodies, during the entire first Round, were "fiery"—built up of the very essence of these fiery lives;—and, although these descended through four globes, or increasingly material states, yet Globe "D" only represented the shadowy prototype of its gross materiality in this Round; so that man's body may be fairly classed as "fiery" throughout, so much did this element predominate. During the next Round it was, let us say, ethereal, and in the next astral, while in this it is molecular or physical. Each of these Rounds lasts, as we have seen, for almost unthinkable periods; and, as the story of man's physical evolution is completely repeated in his intra-uterine life, so is the entire history of his conscious evolution throughout all Rounds repeated swiftly at each incarnation during this Round. In the descending arc, or the first half of the manvantara of seven Rounds, man is simply entangled in matter. The vibration which changes at the end of each of these, under the will of great creative Dhyan Chohans, necessitates his change of vestment independent of his own volition. But in the ascending arc he will have—must have—rewon his divinity, and must take a conscious part in the controlling and molding of not only his physical habitation but his physical environments—his planet. Similarly, at present his reincarnating takes place without his self-conscious volition, but the time must speedily come when he must choose. His devachanic* body, then, corresponds to that of the first Round, and as he descends to earth for another life the body of each succeeding Round will be reconstructed and reoccupied, however briefly, until at his completed reincarnation he finds himself in his present physical habitation.

The correspondence of man's cycles of objective and (relatively) subjective life to manvantaras† and pralayas will now be apparent. When "death" occurs, it disembodies all the hosts of entities incarnated in his physical body, and brings upon them an enforced pralaya, or rest. With certain of these, the pralaya must persist until he reincarnates again, for they are karmically bound to one microcosm alone. Others of a lower order seek other bodies at once, even though they may be reattracted to the same ego at a subsequent incarnation. At any rate, the so-called "death" process sweeps inward until the hour strikes for each entity associated with any microcosm, or body. When the time comes for reincarnation, the ego sweeps downward, awakening from this their pralaya all the numberless hierarchies of lower entities which are to ensoul the "matter" of his body. Descending from fiery matter, these, as we have seen, build for themselves, utilizing the energy of the fiery lives, the ethereal and then the astral forms of former Rounds, and at length reach the physical plane. Here certain entities incarnate as molecules, and, of these, entities a little higher construct cells. Each cell of the human body is a distinct entity, as even science admits. Entities, still higher, synthesize these cells into organs; and finally the human-elemental—the highest of all, and the next to reach the human stage—synthesizes the whole of the body into an avenue fit for the soul to use in its approach to this world. Man's body, physically, differs in no wise from those of the animals. Each of these has its dis-

---

* Devachan—the subjective existence between two earth lives. A state rather than a place, although the latter is a necessity to any entity having form.

† See note page 30.

tinct center of consciousness; and this center, or "soul" of the animal, synthesizes in many instances a body just as complex as is the body of man, and which is, in certain directions, more perfect than his. The great distinction is that in the animal body is an animal "elemental," or one an entire manvantara* behind the human, while in the human body is a "human-elemental," progressed a manvantara farther. The animal elemental—with the exception of certain apes—will not be ready to pass into the human stage for two manvantaras; the human elemental can do so in the next.

The consciousness of the body is below the plane of self-consciousness. As self-consciousness marks the impress of a human soul, and as the consciousness of the body is composed of these innumerable elemental centers of synthesizing consciousness not yet having reached the human stage, it must therefore be below the self-conscious plane. This is the true reason why we are not conscious of the functions of digestion, of waste and repair, growth, and such things. All are done under the supervision of the elementals in our bodies, and we know nothing of them unless they become abnormal in their action, and even then our consciousness of them is faint and often quite absent. But it is perfectly possible, as the microcosm of the macrocosm, for man to transfer his consciousness to these cells; and instances of his doing so, and thus controlling them, are to be found in those Indian Yogis who pierce their flesh with knife-thrusts which immediately heal, etc. Likewise, Christian Scientists at times cure diseases by centering, and—as most Theosophists believe—degrading, the higher, divine consciousness into the performance of purely physical functions which are the normal duties of entities far below the human plane. Disease can often be cured when the will is sufficiently developed by thus transferring the divine, creative consciousness to the physical plane; but the process is in the highest degree abnormal, and must react injuriously in this or succeeding incarnations.

The process of so-called death may be more specifically

---

* Man-perfecting cycle.

described thus: When the "hour" strikes, death begins with the body, and as the soul casts off its successive vestments, it may be said to pass through several. The first of these frees it from the physical cells and the lowest astral body, or Linga Sharira. It now clothes itself for a more or less extended period with a higher astral form, known as the Body of Desires, or Kama Rupa. This after a time it abandons, and remains clothed with its devachanic body until the time comes for it to reincarnate. Another death consists in its reincarnation, or birth here into material existence. These successive deaths are referred to in many scriptures. Even in the Christian Bible we are taught to beware of the "second death," meaning death upon the astral plane. It refers to the possibility of the loss of the human soul through getting enmeshed in the lower Principles, or Quaternary, which normally perish after the death of the body (to be discussed later on).

The dissolution of the body is brought about by other and foreign "lives," or "microbes," when the "fiery lives" abandon it. Our bodies, in common with those of all organized beings, are infested with parasites, both within and without, which are capable of destroying, and will destroy it, after the fiery lives, and with them its "vitality," have departed. But this destruction is the work of parasites. It has been stated in theosophical writings that man is built up of "microbes." Here we must avoid confusing the general use of the word "microbe," from *micro* (small), and *bios* (life), with its technical use in biology and other sciences. In the "Secret Doctrine" it is used in its general sense of "little lives," and we are specially warned against the very confusion which has arisen by the statement that the smallest microbe known to science is as an elephant to a flea compared with these. The microbes of science are all parasites, and abnormal occupants of the human body. This is built up of cells, and cells are not microbes in the scientific use of the term. The success of embalming and preserving mummies depends upon the destruction of these parasites which infest the human body. Their thorough destruction after death will preserve it through countless ages. There was, some time since, the body of an elephant washed out of an ice floe in Russia, which must have been there since the glacial period, and yet the flesh was found untouched by decomposition. Mummies, buried from three to five thousand years since, have portions of the body just as well preserved as though they had been buried only yesterday. Mummification really consists in the destruction of the numerous parasites which infest the human body, and its protection from subsequent invasion by others. Even in life, when the vitality is lowered, these parasites begin to attack the tissues, and multiply at such a rate that they soon transform certain portions of the body into a mass of disease, in which the microbes (parasites) run riot, and cause the dissolution of the whole body unless they are controlled. The death of the body, then, is brought about by the withdrawal from it of the "fiery lives," and its disintegration—quite another thing—through the agency of the microbes which live upon us, and whose attacks we resist during life, because the vitality of the cells, resulting from the presence of the fiery lives, keeps them at bay.

Whence come our bodies physically? Up and through the animal kingdom, undoubtedly, but not from the present animals nor from a common ancestor, even. It is evident that, as the "Secret Doctrine" states, physical man leads the animal kingdom in this Round, for if animals preceded him they ought to be further progressed in evolution than he. The fact that he is farther advanced plainly shows that he came upon this world first, allowing, as we must, common and mutual evolutionary forces afterwards. The "Secret Doctrine," indeed, teaches that he descended from an apelike ancestor; but that ancestor was an astral one, and belonged to the third Round, or that which preceded this.* The centers of consciousness of our physical bodies, known as Lunar Pitris, arrived at the "human-elemental" stage, upon the moon, and came to the earth and constructed for themselves fiery bodies during the first Round. Descending to the ethereal, or second Round, these bodies assumed its qualities, and were formed of ethereal substance. Coming to the astral, or third Round, they built for themselves huge, ape-like bodies of astral matter, which astral bodies, repeated briefly in the third race of this Round, con-

---

*As all evolution is an eternal repetition of the past before a further forward step is taken, so this "ape-like" form was repeated in the third race of this Round.

stitute all the ape-like ancestor man has ever had. During the third Round, his form, being built on subconscious planes and of astral matter, became a kind of huge prototype of that which it afterwards assumed when it descended into the molecular matter of this, the fourth Round. The human-elementals, or Lunar Pitris, which synthesized these forms, came over from the moon when that planet passed into pralaya, and in this manner during the first three and one-half Rounds slowly built up our human bodies into their present shape. At the fourth Round only, these human-animal bodies became capable of receiving and responding to impressions from the Higher Ego, or thinking Soul, and thus enabled the true man to come upon the earth. For man is not the human-elemental, associated with him as the constructor and synthesizer of his body, but the Ray of Manas from the divine Higher Ego, as the result of this incarnation.

The physical cells of which the human body is constructed are the seat of purely physical heredity. The impression of this heredity upon them causes the resemblance to parents. The cells from each parent meet and blend in a most intimate fusion, and their different sources bestow upon them a certain power of variation which causes the child to evolve in the direction of one or the other, and thus affords opportunity for this, which is a necessary portion of evolution. If man came from one parent, he would resemble that parent quite accurately, and each child would be an almost exact reproduction of its parent. But when the origin is from two parents, variation is necessary and is thus provided for. It is, then, along this, the line of physical heredity, that all these resemblances in form and feature, and even in psychic traits, reaches man. The physical is one of the three streams of heredity, flowing into man. The other two will be discussed when their sources are being studied.

If man be the microcosm of the macrocosm, there ought to be exhibited, in his physical organism, evidences of a septenary law, and this is found to be true. His tissues are of seven kinds, pointing to seven distinct hierarchies of entities in its construction. Each of these hierarchies may again be subdivided; making thus forty-nine variants upon the primary seven. These seven tissues are: the neuroglic, connective, areolar, white fibrous, elastic, gelatinous, adenoid, and adipose. The body has seven forms of epithelium: the squamous, spheroid, columnar, transitional, endothelial, and special. There are seven great systems which enter into its construction: the osseous, muscular, nervous, circulatory, reproductive, glandular (including the digestive), and integumentary (including the respiratory). There are seven layers of the skin: epidermis (cuticle), rete mucosum (pigment), papillæ, corium, fat cells, fibrous, and areolar layers. There are seven functions of the skin: limiting, common sensation, heat, cold, pressure, cooling (perspiration), and protective (hair). There are seven divisions of the eye: cornea, aqueous humor, iris, ciliary ligament, lens, vitreous humor, and retina. There are seven layers of the retina: columnar (Jacob's membrane), granular (composed of three distinct layers), nervous layer (consisting of two), and membrana limitans. There are seven divisions of the brain: the medulla oblongata, pons Varolii, crura cerebri, corpora quadrigemina, optic thalami, cerebellum, and cerebrum. There are seven functions of the nervous system: the olfactory, optic, auditory, gustatory, common sensation, and correlating or vegetative. There are seven divisions of the ear: the auditory canal, tympanum, ossicles, semicircular canals, vestibule, cochlea, membranous labyrinth. The blood goes through seven distinct processes in clotting, and in numerous other ways man's physical construction indicates its septenary source. As he is yet in the active process of evolution, there are also very often divisions of five, especially in the chemistry of his body. In fact, such divisions are very numerous throughout man's organism, instances of which are the five senses, five nerves of special sense, five layers of the cornea, etc.

The great lesson to be learned from a study of the body as a Principle, however, is that it inhibits or prevents the conscious functioning of the soul. On its own divine plane—to put it only from a merely mechanical standpoint—the soul uses modes of motion which enable it to record conscious sensations, due to etheric vibrations thousands of times more rapid than those it uses here. In molecular matter, it can see only so many things in a moment. If they pass too rapidly, they are blurred. If it retreat inward, towards its own proper habitation, the vibrations may be almost infinitely more rapid, and it will record them every one, and life, therefore, becomes proportionately fuller and grander. How puerile, then, and how weak is consciousness upon this plane, compared to that of the true home of the soul! How the body limits our senses, and cripples our wings! As we descend from these diviner planes, each new state of matter draws a still heavier veil, so to say, over the eyes of the soul, and it becomes more and more blinded until it reaches the very acme of dullness, and fancies this the only plane of existence, and imagines itself separated from all other human beings. Yet, if it lay off but one of its veils, or "Principles," as in dream, it can pass through experiences in a few moments which would take years in the waking condition. If one could leave his body but for a few minutes, instead of passing into a condition of nothingness, or of losing that which we term life, he would enter upon a life indescribably more vivid. So far from anything having been destroyed or lost, the soul would realize that it had passed into a higher, more perfect state—was functioning upon planes much more subtle—approaching much nearer to the real source of life and being. If this be the result of the change from the molecular to the astral state of matter, how much more will consciousness expand as the soul approaches the center of conscious existence, where consciousness and life are' real!

Let us, then, remember that each of our fellow-men is a divine soul, whose consciousness is limited, whose senses are dulled, whose diviner characteristics are almost destroyed by the gross body it thus temporarily occupies, and we shall then see the reason and the necessity for the exercise towards each other of human sympathy and charity. The character which seems to us so vile is not that of the true soul, but is caused by the body with which it is associated. The qualities which so offend us are but the "qualities" of Matter, in the coils of which the true soul is struggling. These desires arise because they are derived from a plane of existence in which desire is normal—a state whose conscious entities are naturally filled with desire. Man synthesizes these entities into his body, and they transmit their own desires to him; and he, mistaking them for his own, yields to them.

There is a beautiful story told in one of Charles Reade's novels of a prisoner confined in a dungeon, where there was such a perfect exclusion of light that it was impossible for him to have any conception of the passage of time. One could fancy that in a few minutes an hour, or even a day, had passed. So great was the suffering that many came out of it insane. When this prisoner was confined in this dark cell, the chaplain of the prison, knowing the awful effect that such confinement had upon the mind and reason, went to it and rapped upon the outside, in order to let the poor occupant know that on the other side of the walls was a sympathizing, compassionate, human soul. And he tells how the sense of this compassion enabled the prisoner to preserve his reason, and also to pass his period of confinement without suffering. This is similar to the condition of the human soul in these bodies. Therefore, each one of us should constitute himself a compassionate sentinel, standing upon the outside, tapping upon the thick walls of human hearts, letting each know that they have human sympathy, and so feel the hope and trust springing from this. If we remember that each human soul is a divine prisoner, these things which so offend us now will fade away. We will realize that it is not the true person who is doing evil, but only one who has lost control of the passionate body with which he is associated, and our task will be to teach that person to regain his self-control, and thus help to make the whole of humanity happier, nobler, and more divine.

CHAPTER II.

THE LINGA SHARIRA.

THE Second human Principle is called in Sanscrit the Linga Sharira, or Design Body. It is so called because it is upon or within it, as upon a model, that the physical body is constructed. It stands in the relation to the latter that the astral world of the Third Round, or great World Period, stands to this the Molecular Round, or Fourth World Period, and can be best understood by remembering this correspondence or analogy. In those wonderfully deep and comprehensive generalizations of evolution which constitute a portion of the teachings of the Wisdom Religion, the formation of a world is carried backward to points in time compared with which modern geologic figures seem trifling; and it is to the third of these periods, as concerned with the birth and growth of this world, that the "matter" of the Linga Sharira is referred. That is to say, that this world, as has been pointed out in a previous chapter, has passed through an immense period of time in which it was fiery in its constitution, after which, by a change in the rate of the vibration of its "matter" it cooled down into an ethereal state; thence, by means of a still slower rate, its matter became that which we term astral; and, finally, by still another change of vibration, it assumed the coarse, molecular condition of the present great world period, or, as it is technically known in theosophical literature, the Fourth Round. With each of these great world periods, the forms of the entities upon the earth, including man, have of necessity to correspond with the matter of the Round—their bodies being built out of it. The matter of the Third great World Period was astral—that is, its rate of vibration, molecular constitution, and electric, magnetic, and other properties, were such that it assumed this state. During the immense period involved in a "Day of Brahma," a Round, or, scientifically, the length of time in which any particular rate of vibration remains the keynote or dominating motion in the matter of a world, this astral world was occupied by all the hosts of entities which we now find upon the earth, but of course in a very much less progressed state.

Like glazier's putty, "matter" becomes more pliable, more responsive to thought, the more it is used; and so this astral matter has, by its long use during an entire Round, become so plastic that thought-forms are instantly constructed of it, as is experienced every night in dreams. For the forms and scenes perceived in dreams are actual and real; are constructed by the ideative force of the imagination out of this same plastic astral matter; and, for the brief period during which man's feeble will holds them intact, are as real and as stable as any material forms within the Cosmos. The very changes which are observed in fleeting or panoramic dreams are possible because of, and due to, this ability of astral matter to respond to the vagaries of even the dreaming imagination, though this be quite uncontrolled by the higher mind.

But with the change of vibration at the close of the Third great World Period, appeared molecular matter as we perceive it to-day; just as a change of temperature—which is but a change of vibration—in a saline solution will cause solid crystals to appear in that which was before transparent. Such crystals represent the exact vibratory change which has taken place in the entire fluid; or, to resort to scientific terms again, the amount of heat which has become "latent" in the process. For it must not be understood that all the substance of the earth changes its rate of vibration at the end of each great evolutionary period, or that all the energies concerned in its construction become "latent," except those comparatively feeble molecular forces with which we are familiar. Only a small portion, compared with the entire mass of matter, does so, and only a very minute portion of the forces involved pass into molecular activities. Thus, the earth still has the fiery, ethereal, and astral globes of preceding world periods; each globe being the mother liquid, so to speak, out of which the lower one has crystallized. All these states interpenetrate, or are in a condition, as again expressed in terms of science, of co-adunition, and constitute the seven globes of our earth chain.

The origin of the Linga Sharira of Man may now, perhaps, be

better understood. The changes of vibration which constitute and determine these great world periods, or Rounds, are due, we are taught, to that which is termed Monadic impulse, or to the almost, if not quite, direct action of that eternal Motion which is described in Eastern philosophy as the "Great Breath." In its origin and essence, it is alike unknowable; as finite beings we are limited entirely to studies of its finite modes of motion. But of itself this Monadic motion is incapable of producing form, and must be understood as that of the Universal or Absolute Monad; that Unknowable base upon which all the so-called properties of matter as well as the infinite states of consciousness within the Universe alike rest, for Spirit and Matter are but aspects of the One Absolute, Causeless Cause, and, as such aspects, are both conditioned and finite. That portion of the Absolute which is at the base of a human soul is called the human monad; and this monad, having descended into the sphere of finite or conditioned existence, in, let us say the fire-mist stage of evolution, finds itself incapable of constructing a form. To quote the "Secret Doctrine":*

"For the Monad, or Jiva, *per se*, can not even be called spirit. It is a Ray, a breath of the Absolute, or the Absoluteness, rather; and the Absolute Homogeneity, having no relations with the conditioned and relative finiteness, is unconscious on our plane. Therefore, besides the material which will be needed for its future human form, the monad requires (a) a spiritual model or prototype for that material to shape itself into, and (b) an intelligent consciousness to guide its evolution and progress, neither of which is possessed by the homogeneous monad or by senseless though living matter."

It is at this point that Eastern Wisdom solves our perplexity by its theory of emanations. At each great change in the vibration of matter, advantage of the change is taken by high creative beings to clothe themselves with the matter which has thus taken on new qualities, both because of such change of vibration and because of these creative beings having bestowed upon the entities which ensoul it a portion of their own essence by emanation. Such creative Beings are the source of all forms in the so-called "lower" kingdoms, as they are, indeed, in all nature.

---
*Vol. I, p. 247.

The form of Man, then, during all the Rounds preceding this was given by high or low creative beings who have the power to cause the "matter" of each Period or Round to assume definite designs. This is the key to the numerous Pitris or "fathers," which we find accredited to Man in such apparently confusing and profuse perplexity in the "Secret Doctrine." Each appropriate Hierarchy gave to his Monad the form it occupied during that particular World Period; and in doing so imparted, just as the magnet imparts its own magnetism to non-magnetic iron, a portion of their own essence. This imparted essence, again, is a key to a portion of the still more confusing array of "Principles," which seem to be a part, and still not a part, of man's complex being. It is, however, this complexity entering into his constitution which makes Man the microcosm of the macrocosm; for as every entity in the universe either "is, was, or prepares to become a man," so do all the creative intelligences, all the so-called "forces" of nature, aid and conspire to make Man what he now is and what he may become, by a long evolutionary association with (thus bestowing their own essence upon) him.

In the Third great World Period certain entities, whom we may term "human elementals," and whom, we are told, had arrived at this stage during the course of an evolution upon the moon, associated themselves with the still unconscious human monad, and constructed for it, out of astral matter, an astral body—the prototype of the present Linga Sharira as well as the model said to be needed by the "too spiritual" monad. They remained associated with the human monad, and constituted Man's chief principle during the entire Third Round, and are still so associated with him. But their office of modeling for him a body of even astral matter has ceased. His molecular body is, as we have seen, built up of "pranic lives," and by the "Spirits of the Earth," we are further told. Another and very much higher class of entities—our own Higher Egos—have taken charge of the duty of furnishing a new Linga Sharira at each birth, and the office of the "Lunar Pitris" has become, at best, only mechanical. They are now the servitors of the real Man, and must follow the designs laid down by the true Man, the Higher Ego.

The design body, the Linga Sharira, then, is a "thought body" of the Higher Ego, the true man, impressed first, and before the physical body is formed, upon the plastic astral matter of the Third Round. The Higher Ego, can not so quickly impress physical matter, for this is yet too new, hard, and unyielding. But the changes which follow, in the human form and features, upon a radical change of thought give a promise and prophesy of those powers which it is slowly acquiring, and of which we shall see the completed fruition at the close of this Manvantara, when the whole earth will be but the reflection of perfected human Thought. Meantime, astral matter is utilized because of its plasticity, and into the model so furnished the senseless—upon this plane—"lower lives" build Man's form.

What is the *modus operandum* of the actual construction of the Linga Sharira? The Higher Ego can not be said to construct it consciously — or, at least, not self-consciously. It is certainly a creative act upon the part of the soul returning to incarnation, but one not exercised as yet self-consciously by the vast majority of the human race. For the exact copying of purely physical tendencies as to size and shape, or of low psychic tricks of gesture, etc., show that there are other forces at work besides the pure, creative energy of the Soul. The ordinary child is almost an exact copy of its physical parents, showing that these, too, have had their undoubtedly subconscious influence in determining the new form, and that this influence has been a most potent one. The explanation lies in the fact of physical heredity: that there are in our bodies to-day, as Weissmann declares, cells which have never died since the world began. These cells are impressed, are, indeed, the very record of man's physical past, and carry in their essence an almost irresistible tendency to exactly repeat the old physical structure, as is seen in those lowly forms where physical heredity is almost the sole modifying agency. Nature opposes this tendency upon the higher planes of her kingdoms by interposing cells from two differing parents, thus providing a physical basis for that necessary variation which evolutionary progress demands—and which necessity is the true reason for the evolutionary separation into sexes;—and, secondly, the further modifying influence of the ideation of the returning soul and of its physical parents upon the mental plane. It is along this line of unstable equilibrium that all evolutionary progress takes place, and man's wonderfully complex nature affords it its highest field of activity. Thus, the initiative force—that of the returning soul—calls into activity the "fiery lives," and the first or ideal thought-form upon their plane is constructed. But as this tends to repeat itself upon lower and lower planes of Man's being, as his Ego descends to more and more material planes in the successive steps of its reincarnation, more and more modifying and obstructive energies are encountered. The subconscious thought of the parents is one source of these; then come the *Skandhas*—sleeping or "latent" entities representing man's passional and emotional nature as expressed or evolved in past lives, which demand modifications that shall better express their qualities. All these are at work on the plastic astral model; and when this finally encounters the lower cell lives, carrying the impress of the experience and "habits" of myriads of ages, the Linga Sharira succumbs: the divine consciousness of the soul has sunk too deeply into matter to make its energies a potent factor; and the imperfect human form, largely the repetition of its physical ancestry, is the result. The astral model, also, is the reason for the perpetuation of species throughout all nature. In the lower kingdoms it, having been, so to speak, permanently molded by the ideation of the Creative Entities for the Round, tends, as we have seen, to an almost exact repetition of the same form. As evolution, however, pushes the entity upward in the scale of being, the complex factors, which we have pointed out as modifying influences upon the human Linga Sharira, slowly come into play; sex differentiation occurs, and, one by one, all the various modifying evolutionary forces exert their activites. There is no possible reason why two cells almost identical in form should differentiate, the one into the form of a delicate fern, and the other into that of a giant sequoia, except that this ideal astral form persists, and is an actual model into which, just as in the human instance, the forms of all the entities of the lower kingdoms of nature are built.

In studying the nature and functions of the Linga Sharira more specifically, we are taught that it dissipates, step by step, with the matter of the body. This is because of the withdrawal after death from it, as well as from the physical body, of the "fiery lives," which gave both their vitality. This vitality, from one—a purely mechanical—standpoint, is supplied by the "fiery lives" becoming latent, or changing the rate of their vibration. It is analogous to the disappearance of heat by crystallization, etc., upon lower planes. But in this case the latency is enforced by the unconsciously exercised will of the reincarnating entity. Its *tanha*, or desire for physical existence, causes the "fiery lives" to yield to it, and it synthesizes the force so derived into the construction and preservation of its body. During life the Linga Sharira is said to be the vehicle of Prana, or the Life Principle; but its connection with this will be best studied when we take up the latter Principle. It is capable of passing out of the body during life, and in such case has the peculiar power of attracting to itself physical atoms from the surrounding atmosphere in such quantities as to reproduce a replica of the human form. In certain instances this projection is, no doubt, the seat of the soul itself In any case, the real physical body appears languid and apathetic during the absence of this its astral counterpart. This power of attracting to itself physical atoms resident in the atmosphere is the cause of the Linga Sharira being so often seen by people who are not clairvoyant. Given a death in which the dying person has intently thought of some distant dear one, and the Linga Sharira has often been known to go, under the impulse of this thought force, to that person or distant place, and actually appear as a more or less faint duplicate or image of the dying person. It is often noticed as a vague violet light, or violet mist, over the graves of the recently dead, and also in these cases is seen by non-clairvoyants, and must of course be composed of matter capable of being seen by the physical eye. Such visible matter is, in the opinion of the writer, an attempt at reincarnation, by reclothing itself, temporarily and faintly, with physical atoms floating in the atmosphere, and is the result of the force of habit due to its life-long association with a physical body.

This power, or innate tendency, rather, to surround itself with physical or molecular matter is no doubt at the basis of most of the "materializations" which take place at spiritualistic "seances." The Linga Sharira of the medium leaves, or oozes out of, the body; the very capacity for doing which constitutes one a "medium." Once outside the body, under the strong, impelling desire of the medium, or of some of the sitters, the Linga Sharira becomes molded into the form of some departed person, and then attracts to itself a sufficient amount of physical atoms to appear as solid flesh. It has, in fact, become a solid, though temporary, thought-form of some person present among the sitters, and is possessed of the limited intelligence which such thought-forms are capable of exhibiting. So powerful may be the so-called "materialization," so deceiving the electric and magnetic forces involved, that such "spooks" have all the appearances of a solid physical body; have actual weight, though this has been known to vary by many pounds within a very few moments in the same "spook," upon being weighed. But this change in weight is doubtless due more to an interference with the laws of attraction and repulsion, of which gravity is a phase, than with any real accession or departure of actual physical molecules. Many of these physical molecules are drawn from the sitters present, as the exhaustion of those who are at all mediumistic, after such a seance, amply testifies. The decomposition at the close of the seance of molecules thus withdrawn from the bodies of sitters is the cause of that peculiarly offensive "grave odor" which is always perceived when a genuine materialization has taken place. Of course, the Linga Sharira will not explain all the phenomena of materializations; it is only its part in this process that now concerns us. A Linga Sharira thus extruded and materialized is capable of being injured by blows or violence of any sort, in which case, upon its returning to the body, the marks of injuries thus inflicted upon it will be repeated upon the medium's body, and reappear as actual fleshly injuries. This is because, being the model of the physical form, the real supporter of the physical cells, when it, the model, is altered the tendency of the physical cells to flow into the new design is almost irresistible, and in this manner actually causes the repetition of injuries upon the physical body. This fact is known in spiritualistic parlance as "repercussion," and the relation of the Linga Sharira to the physical form fully explains this otherwise inexplicable phenomenon. The capacity to thus project the Linga Sharira is possessed in a greater or lesser degree by mediums and seers, and, Mr. Wm. Q. Judge declares, by the hysterical, cataleptic and scrofulous.*

The organs of sense, the real centers for seeing, hearing, tasting, and smelling, are located in the Linga Sharira, the proof of which was pointed out in the lecture upon the physical body. Yet, although man has thus the capacity for seeing, hearing, tasting, and smelling, or, in other words, of exercising all his senses upon the astral plane, his capacity for so doing is almost *nil* while in the physical body, and is exceedingly limited even when disconnected from this by death. The exercise of the astral senses during life constitutes a low form of clairvoyance and clairaudience, which is much sought after by those ignorant of their own nature, and to whom such glimpses into the unseen are taken for communications from some "heavenly" sphere. There is, no doubt, something which corresponds to sense-organs in astral bodies much higher than the Linga Sharira; but as man's soul recedes inward these become less and less capable of conveying to him external impressions, because of their not yet being sufficiently perfected by use. It will, no doubt, be a portion of his evolution to perfect these interior sense-organs during future World Periods—to become self-conscious, and to exteriorise these now subjective planes in a manner exactly similar to that in which he objectivises his present physical environment. Such sense-organs and astral bodies, composed of finer grades of matter than is the Linga Sharira, correspond to the great hiatus in vibration which lies between the waves of sound, or those which affect man's sense of hearing, and those of light, which appeal to his organs of vision. Thus, sound-waves travel at the rate of about thirteen hundred feet a minute, and are of variable length, while waves of light travel at the rate of 184,000 miles a second, and have a wave length of about 1-52,000 of an inch. Between the sense of sound, said to be the result of molecular motion, and that of sight,

---
*Ocean of Theosophy.

attributed to "ethereal" vibrations, there is evidently an immense gulf of hidden sense potentialities. In the vibrations of light, also, there is evidently an unbroken continuity of successively more rapid vibrations above the violet ray, as proven by the chemical changes produced, and below the red ray, with which man's color perception ceases in this direction. So of all his senses. There are sounds which he can not hear; there are substances which have for him no taste. Into such realms of nature interior senses, located in finer, more ethereal astral bodies, must some time project him. Thus we are told, in the "Secret Doctrine," that ether, now so hypothetical and unreal, will become visible in the air towards the end of this globe Round or World Period. This does not mean that ether is not in the atmosphere now, but that we are unable to perceive it; and prophesies, not the condensation of the ether, but the evolution of finer qualities of perception in our sense-organs.

The condition of human consciousness at death can also be best understood, perhaps, by an examination of the correspondence between the separation of the lower human Principles and the changes of vibration which limit and define a World Period. Thus, at the death of the body, a period which corresponds to the termination of this Fourth Round, or molecular World Period, the life Principle retreats inward, and the body is left to decay, precisely as a dead world in space decays when its higher Principles are also withdrawn, as we see in the case of the dead moon, and of those recently dissipated intra-Mercurial planets which science suspects, but of which it so vainly seeks evidence. The soul then becomes six-principled for a brief period—has for its outermost clothing the Linga Sharira. But it soon detaches itself from this vehicle, for the Linga Sharira as well as the body is molecular. Then the Ego clothes itself with an astral form of finer matter; or of that of a higher rate of vibration, and becomes a five-principled being. That is to say, that all the "lives" with which it was associated upon the material plane pass into Pralaya, or latency, and no longer disturb the soul by their activities. Prana also disappears—which will be more fully explained when dealing with that Principle. So long as there is the faintest connection between the soul and the Linga Sharira so long is the latter capable of disturbing, to a degree at least, the repose of the soul. This is one reason for cremation, aside from other purely sanitary reasons.

Like all states of matter, the astral plane of substance has its seven grades, the lowest of which passes directly into the physical, or visible, molecular condition, while its higher States grade upward into vibrations capable of affording all those vestments of the soul which constitute its many "Astral Bodies." There is—there can be—no abrupt break between the vibrations of one state and that of another. They are as continuous as life itself. Our sense-organs may and do mark them off into distinct planes, as when the sense of sight records one rate of vibration as red, and one, but slightly higher, as orange; but there is no point at which we can say that here, precisely, the red ceases and the orange begins. So with the after-death states and the vestments of the soul—a portion of the Linga Sharira remains entangled within the cells of the body, and dissipates *pari passu* with it. Another portion oozes out of the body, forming a wraith or duplicate of this, and also affording a very transient vestment for the soul. This, after being abandoned by the Ego, is, no doubt, re-attracted to the latter, and also dissipates, step by step, with it. Still another portion is used by the kama-manasic, or lower, mind, or Principle, to clothe itself with a thought-form, which afterwards fades, with the cessation of the activities of this, into the "spook," the abode of the kama-rupa, or that human elemental which is the synthesizer of man's purely animal body, as it continues, for a more prolonged period, its existence as an independent entity in kama-loka. The successive abandonment of these vestments, or their vibrations, ceasing to possess the power to command the soul's attention, constitute the key to the after-death states of consciousness. While in the Linga Sharira proper, the state of the soul is that of calm. Stupefied by the great change in its environment as to vibration, would, perhaps, better express its condition. But as it recovers from this shock, as it gathers itself together, so to speak, and particularly after, by its own mental effort, it constructs for itself a body of astral matter containing the impress, habits, and desires of the life it has just quitted, it is itself again. It is in kama-loka—in that uncanny region where it is still under the influence of earth desires, thrust upon its consciousness by the vigorous vibrations of this which has been well termed the "body of desire." For it is the seat of desire during life, and still more so after the death of the body. But, let us suppose that these earth-tending desires are not fed or renewed vicariously by any foolish medium, to her own and the soul's hurt; then they slowly cease, and the soul falls asleep to all vibration except that of its own proper "thought body," in which "to will is to create, and to think is to see." This is its "heaven," its Devachan, its rest; a state, from the standpoint of vibration alone, caused and made possible by the cessation of all the activities or vibrations of the lower bodies which it has cast off, or to which it has become indifferent. No vibrations reach it now but the very highest and most spiritual of its past life—those unselfish, altruistic, and spiritual enough to make an impress upon and be recorded within the tablets of the true soul. The hierarchies of turbulent, passionate lives with which he was associated while in the physical body, and whose imperious voices he so ignorantly mistook for the demands of his own soul, have been hushed; he is again at the fountain source of his true being, drinking again of the waters of everlasting life. In Devachan—

"The sin and shame, the woe and misery
 Will all have faded. Memory's drifting ships
Will cast the gall and wormwood in the sea,
 And bring sweet wines alone into our longing lips."

Here the soul remains, enjoying all the felicities of its own divinity, until the impulse of its spiritual nature is exhausted, when it again bows to the law of its own evolution; again yields to the sway of the "fiery lives" as they force it once more into the realms of sensuous existence; constructs for itself a new Linga Sharira, into and upon which a new physical body is builded, and—takes up its old-life tasks again.

CHAPTER III.

PRANA.

WHILE a portion of man's Principles are derived from, or are the very essence of, beings higher than he, there are others which are not so derived, but which seem to root in the very Absolute itself. They are as direct aspects of the Absolute in man (the microcosm) as they are in the Universe (or macrocosm). Such are Atma, man's seventh; Buddhi, his second; and Prana, the third Principle. Viewed from a purely physical standpoint, all life upon the earth is derived, primarily or secondarily, from the sun, which seems to be a great storehouse for all forms of force, or modes of motion. Heat, light, electricity, magnetism, "vital" force—all radiate apparently from this great center of Cosmic energy. Blot the sun out of the heavens, and this earth would, in a very few days at the most, float aimlessly in space, a huge, frozen, lifeless corpse.

There are, of course, other, and very greatly modifying, conditions which affect, favorably or unfavorably, the continuance of life here, such as the inclination of the earth's axis to the sun, the percentage of moisture in the atmosphere, etc.; but as these are but secondary causes, at best, whose primaries depend upon the sun for their modifying influence, the latter may be said to be truly the giver of physical life to the earth. This life seems to be the result of, or due to, motion or vibration, which latter is transmitted to the earth by means of a medium which science conjectures to be its "ether," and reaches the earth in the form of vibrations. It is interesting to note how exactly the conclusions of science, as to the manner in which these vibrations reach and react upon the molecular matter of the earth, repeat unconsciously the occult formula as to the mode in which Prana, or the Life Principle, is related to the human body. Just as the vibrations from the sun are transmitted by an intermediary agent— the ether,—so does Occultism declare that Prana reaches the body through and by means of an astral or ethereal body—the Linga Sharira.

But one must not fall into the error of confusing these vibrations in the ether with Prana, or the Life Principle itself. That would be to say that the vibrations set up in the Linga Sharira by Prana constituted the essence of Prana itself, and would land one in the purely materialistic theory of the mechanical origin of all life. [Prana roots in Absolute Motion—in the force or will-aspect of the Causeless Cause.] The Sun is the active agent in its storing, and the "ether" or some intermediary substance in its transmission to the earth, but the Life Essence itself is something quite apart from the mechanical vibrations which transmit it, or exhibit its presence

It is but the effects of Prana acting in the atoms of astral or ethereal matter that science is vainly striving to materialize in its hypothesis of the ether. In its real essence or nature, Prana is, of course, undiscoverable; for that which Occultists classify as Prana is but the phenomenal manifestation of the universal Life Principle acting upon the plane of molecular substance. This universal Life Principle may be said to be one of three hypostases of the Absolute; which hypostases appear to our perception as Motion, Substance, and Consciousness.] Into one or other of these infinite aspects of the Absolute, or Causeless Cause, every finite phenomenon finally resolves itself. They *are* the Absolute as this is reflected in Time and Space. They are, as we have seen, never dissociated under manifested conditions—the only ones which finite minds are capable of comprehending;—can not even be thought of separately. Consciousness, often spoken of as Spirit, is at the base of all ideation, perception, and sensation. Substance furnishes the material substratum for all form, and is the medium in which Motion (will or force) is clothed, as well as the vehicle for the manifestation of Consciousness. Motion divested of all other attributes represents the Universal Life Principle in the Universe—is Life, in its very essence, it would seem; for if motion ceases upon any plane, so-called death upon that plane occurs at once, and the entity which was clothed in the substance in which motion has thus ceased must retreat or follow the life vibration to other and inner planes. If we look upon the human monad as a ray from the Absolute, and as therefore containing potentially the three aspects or hypostases of this, then its conscious aspect may be thought of, or distinguished, as Atma; its Substance aspect as Buddhi, or the Akasa, or "mulaprakriti," of Eastern philosophy; and its active or life aspect as Jiva. Indeed, this seems to be the sense in which these two Sanscrit words, "Jiva" and "Atma," are used in much theosophic literature. It is only when Jiva, or the manifested aspect of Absolute Life or motion, reaches the molecular plane of the Universe that it is termed Prana, and is then classed as the third human Principle.

It is evident that it is no more a Principle in man than it is in the rock, the vegetable, the animal, or in any form composed of molecules. It is simply the aspect of Jiva, the universal life Principle, upon this, the molecular plane of the universe. Life is everywhere; in every conceivable point in space it is potentially, if not actually, present. Being the motion or will-aspect of the unknowable Causeless Cause, it must pervade every possible region in all the inconceivable abysses of space. Therefore, when Prana, that aspect of the universal life Principle acting in molecular substance, passes from form to form of such matter, it simply abandons one, at the so-called "death" of this, to associate itself with another; assuming during the brief interval (if, indeed, there really be an interval) its jivic or universal life-aspect again. For Prana of itself is unable to construct a molecular form, or even to maintain or preserve one beyond the cycle of the entity which has synthesized it and so made a molecular form possible. Just as we have seen in our study of the Linga Sharira that the human monad is unable to create (synthesize) for itself a form, but that conscious entities have to do this for it, so also this Pranic aspect of the universal life Principle is guided in its workings in lower forms by entities who synthesize or construct such lower "lives" into forms, and control and direct the forces of Prana so long as this association continues. Thus, Prana, from another point of view, may be described as the force of the "fiery lives"—the first and "fiery" differentiations of the homogeneous substance of planes above the molecular, and even the atomic—which, synthesized and coördinated in a manner to be described, builds into the form of cells the lower Pranic molecular "lives." These cells, again, are synthesized into an appropriate form by the entity thus swinging into the objective arc of its life cycle, and Jiva now becomes Prana, because its energy is directed to and acts within the molecular plane of substance.

But the action of the "fiery lives," thus sweeping downwards, or (to coin a term) molecular-wards, would be chaotic, as we have seen, and quite unintelligent as regards this plane, were not this action directed to the production of a particular form by the molds or models cut and shaped in astral matter (which matter we have also seen when dealing with the Linga Sharira to have the quality of responding instantaneously to thought) by the action of ideation. The endeavor was made, in the chapter referred to, to point out the source of and the various modifying influences acting upon the Linga Sharira, or the model for the human form. This guiding influence thus exerted upon the action of the "fiery lives" again illustrates how complex is the origin of man's form even, and how all his Principles act and react upon and within each other in completing his many-sided nature. The withdrawing of the Higher Ego does not release the synthesis of Prana necessary to the maintenance of the human form; it only leaves man an intellectual animal; but the withdrawal of the "Animal Soul" of the older classifications, or of that (human) elemental which synthesizes the action of Prana in the human form, exactly as lower elementals do in the animal and vegetable kingdoms, means the surrender of the human form to the uncontrolled action of the lower lives, who soon tear and rend it asunder. Then Prana as a human Principle disappears, which is to say that the coördinated action of the "fiery lives" disappears. Prana does not disappear; its activity is now greater than before; but, being no longer synthesized and coördinated, causes the so-called death and disintegration of the body. It is thus evident that, as thought has the power to cause substance to take form, so have all centers of consciousness, from atom-soul to god, the power to receive from, or to assimilate out of, the unknowable Fount of Life enough of Jiva or Prana, as the case may be, to bestow vitality—using Western and highly inaccurate phraseology—upon, or, according to Eastern philosophy, to synthesize it in, their respective bodies, and that when they abandon these material forms they withdraw this synthesizing influence or power. But such abandoned forms have still within them the Prana or Life Principle appropriate to a lower plane of consciousness.

This power to thus assimilate, or, as Mr. Judge* puts it, to "secrete," Prana out of the great ocean of Jiva, which every conscious entity from atom to god possesses, is one derived, no doubt, from the very Absolute itself; results, indeed, because life (or motion) substance and consciousness are always associated—are but aspects of the one indivisible, omnipresent Absolute. Life and force, or motion, are indissolubly associated; and when the force of modern science becomes "latent" it only means that the eternal motion has changed its rate of vibration—has passed into a lower plane of substance as well as of consciousness. Life is thus seen to be one, indestructible and continuous, and death but a change in the conditions of its manifestation. The third human principle is shown to be a universal one; and is called Prana merely to distinguish one field of the operation of this universal Principle.

Let us now look for a moment at the question of Life from its purely physical aspect. Materialists have in vain sought for its mysterious origin in the "matter" which constitutes their god. For many years spontaneous generation, or abiogenesis, as it is scientifically termed, was universally believed in, and was an immense support to the materialistic hypothesis. If it were, indeed, possible for blindly working forces to push inorganic or lifeless matter up out of the mineral into the vegetable and animal kingdoms, then the origin of life and consciousness might, with some show of reason, be attributed to certain properties of matter—which is the materialistic claim. But later and still more "scientific" researches, by Pasteur and others, have completely disproven the spontaneous-generation theory, so that one of the most important of the strongholds of materialism has been demolished to its very foundations. Science has now to look beyond the mere properties of matter if it would find even a working

---

*Ocean of Theosophy.

hypothesis to explain the origin of life. And this, indeed, it is beginning to do. Many of its greatest exponents, including such devoted adherents as Huxley and Hæckel, admit the impossibility of abiogenesis at present, but claim that in distant periods of the world's evolution there was a time when the magnetic, electric, temperature, and other conditions prevailing upon the earth were such that that which has since become impossible was possible then; that then matter did respond to force, and the organic appear out of the inorganic—using these terms, of course, in the older scientific sense. Such scientists are very nearly in accord with the theosophic theory of evolution. For Theosophy teaches that the door for monadic ingress was closed at the middle of this Round; which, put in scientific terms, means that at that period spontaneous generation ceased, because of the earth having reached its lowest condition of materiality—one so low, indeed, that spirit or thought is unable to act upon it directly, but must approach it through the medium of the finer, more plastic astral matter, of the preceding Round or World Period. But as to the nature of the force causing their so-called spontaneous generation, these thinkers are as far from the theosophic conception as are the poles asunder. For with them the appearance of form is, after all, but blind force taking the direction of the least resistance; while for Theosophists astral forms followed by molecular ones is the action of force representing the will of conscious thinking entities, which entities are the real creators of all form. Blind force taking the direction of either the least or greatest resistance never has produced nor never can produce form. So deeply philosophical is the theosophic conception of the origin of life that it is recognized that even the Spiritual Monad, after its differentiation within the Absolute and its start downward through its cycle of manifested existence, is still unable, as we have seen, to construct for itself a form, but needs the assistance of thinking entities, farther differentiated and so relatively lower than itself, to accomplish this. Theosophists, indeed, recognize that there was a time when spontaneous generation (but not that of the scientists) was a universal fact and factor throughout nature. This period is represented by the Third Round, when the earth was composed of the astral matter previously described, and the first half of this, or the Fourth Round.

The type of all life upon the earth is the cell, and it is from cells that all the wilderness of forms which we see in nature about us are built up. The earth itself represents, as do all earths and suns, but an immense cell made up of an infinite number of lesser cells, and stars and planets, even in their form, conform to the cellular or spherical model.

Abiogenesis, or the spontaneous generation of the scientists, having been disproved, and Occultism declaring that the door for monadic ingress closed at the middle of the Fourth Round, it remains, then, to examine the nature of the real physical basis of life, or the means by which physical forms are transmitted from parent to offspring. The theory most in accord with the occult teaching, and one, indeed, which explains purely physical heredity correctly, is that of Weissmann. He declares that there is one cell, formed by the union of the male and female plasm, from divisions and modifications of which the entire human form is built up. That is to say, that every cell in the human body has a minute portion of this original cell, and that by means of the presence of the matter of this primordial cell in every cell of the body physical heredity is carried forward. These primordial cells represent the completed type of life on their plane, for they are sevenfold in their constitution. They have a germinal spot, a nucleolus, a nucleus, a membrane limiting the nucleus, a cell plasm, and an inner and outer membrane of the cell proper. Such perfect cells, then, are capable of being used, through various modifications of them, in order to build up the multiform tissues of the body; and it is the various subdivisions of these germinal cells with which the hierarchies of elementals clothe themselves in building up the human form. Thus, each living being, of whatever degree, now clothed in flesh has within it certain cells which have never died since the time that the primordial "matter" of this earth yielded to the primordial impress of "spirit," or the modifying associations of spiritual entities seeking re-embodiment. Such cells are, as Weissmann points out, relatively eternal; and are handed down from parent to offspring, and with them comes all the modifying influences of past associations as to form and physical functions. There is little if any doubt but that any entity now upon the earth has been here many, many times before, clothed in a similar material form to that which it now occupies, and which it only very slowly modifies under the stress of its necessity for developing new avenues for consciousness. The real entity, however, is concealed, and its presence only revealed by the material form it occupies, and which is but the outward expression of such an inner presence.

The physical basis of life, then, is these non-dying cells, handed down from parent to offspring, and bringing with them the impress of the entire physical characteristics of both parents, which meet and blend in the new form so provided. The spiritual plasm or force is that synthesized by the reincarnating entity, whose function it is, as we have seen, to control the action of Prana in the lower hierarchial "lives," so that this form can be constructed and maintained.

The maintenance of the integrity of the physical form is effected by a constant synthesizing effort upon the part of the inner entity. It is the expression of its will to live; the sum of its desires for sensuous existence. The force, which is but a phase of will-power, is exerted subconsciously in all instances. Thought can and does modify this force; but few among mortals know how to direct it. Sickness is thus due to failure on the part of the entity to control or synthesize the action of Prana in its organism. The natural action of the "fiery lives" is always at war with this synthesizing effort, and unless the man has cultivated his will strongly in this direction very little suffices to turn the balance. When one has cultivated or strengthened his will to live in past lives, in this one he will be said to be full of "vitality,"—in other words, Prana will be under his control,—while the ordinary man will be threatened by foes, both within and without. Any violation of the laws of nature, any infection or injury—the thousand pitfalls which surround man's footsteps—disturbs the balance of Prana, and shortens his life. So universally is life shortened by our ignorance and willfulness that its span, which we are taught, ought to cover some four hundred years, does not average a tenth of this period.

One of the chief foes to the proper action of Prana is to be found in the parasites, or "microbes," which have their normal habitation in and upon man's tissues, as they also have in and upon those of every entity, however minute. These are the active agents in the final disintegration of the body when death occurs—as was stated in the chapter upon the body. But these microbes, as we have also seen, must not be confused with the "lives" from which the human body is constructed. The microbes of science are true parasites, and are never built into the tissues of the body as constructive material. The microbes spoken of in the "Secret Doctrine" are the minute "lives" of which the tissues of the body are built up, and are classified in the "Secret Doctrine" as belonging to "the first and lowest subdivision—that of material Prana, or Life." When we consider that there are well-known and well-studied bacteria which it requires a microscope with a magnifying power of several hundred of diameters to disclose, the excessive minuteness of these molecularly clad lives can begin to be appreciated. Every entity with a form independently constructed has these its natural enemies, and the human form is no exception. All diseases which have been and are being traced to germs—a large and constantly increasing class—are due to the restraining action of the entity, working through the "fiery lives," being inhibited. All diseases of any kind are due, as has been pointed out, to the same cause; and all true remedies either act as germicides upon the microbes, or as centers of modifying vibration in organs in which the action of Prana is so disturbed. The selective action not only of remedies, but also of the tissues themselves in taking their proper nutriment out of a common and highly heterogeneous stock of food, is due to an unison or chord between the Pranic vibration of such remedy or food and the normal or abnormal vibration, as the case may be, in the healthy or diseased tissues, which they thus help in the one case to build up or in the other to restore to the normal function.

The "fiery lives" through which the Pranic energy is transmitted give of their own essence to the lower molecular lives, which they thus build up by merging, as it were, into these lower lives for the time being. The process would seem to be similar to that which takes place when heat becomes latent, or a modification of vibration. Changes in the vibratory action of its molecules will cause the vapor of water, for instance, to pass by successive steps into the liquid and then into the solid state. So the Pranic vibrations of the "fiery lives," or of those entities constituting the ultimate division of matter within the Cosmos, pass by a similar modification of vibration into these molecular lives or states. But this action of the "fiery lives" is also subject to the universal law of cycles, and it is this cyclic action which sets a limit to life upon the molecular plane, despite the will of the Ego to live. Thus the body of even an Adept would yield to this law of periodicity when the downward sweep of the "fiery lives" came to its normal close. This fact alone negatives such theories of prolonged life as are set forth, for example, in Bulwer Lytton's "Zanoni." While the normal length of life is stated to be very much longer than that of the ordinary individual, still, there is a limit to continuance in a physical body, and this limit is determined by the action of Prana itself, as manifested in these "fiery lives."

Without, then, attempting to solve the ultimate origin or nature of life, which loses itself in the abysses of the Unknowable, we can, in a mechanical sort of way, trace the action and understand the nature of Prana in its working in our bodies, as well as in nature about us. Never losing sight of the fact that motion (force), substance, and consciousness are always associated upon this plane of manifestation, we can peceive that the coming into being of the "fiery lives" is the result—in one aspect, and that grossly materialistic—of a change in the rate of vibration in inner, or to us subjective, or spiritual spheres. It is the descent of "spirit" into "matter," for by this change of vibration that aspect of the Absolute which appears to us as matter becomes ascendant. Thus, the "fiery lives" will represent the first ripple upon the ocean of manifestation, from our point of view. They may seem as gross as the granite rock to beings higher than we. And, mechanically again, they represent the higher, spiritual vibrations becoming latent, or potential only, upon this almost homogeneous plane. But the vibrations of these "fiery lives," thus limited and bound by differentiation are almost of infinite rapidity, compared with those which they assume when they again descend into the still lower material latency of the "lives" and "matter" out of which our bodies are constructed.

The universe is thus seen to be one vast laboratory of life, wherein this mysterious essence is working in infinite variations, through infinitely different, yet harmonious, modes of manifestation. We are ourselves but as drops in this infinite ocean of existence; our very bodies composed of innumerable lower lives, in the one universe of Being. As we act in relation to these lower lives, so will they react upon us in our next association with them, for there is but small doubt that we are associated for almost an infinite length of time with the same Pranic lives, which, again and again, build bodies similar to those in which we now find ourselves. Therefore, the lesson to be learned from the study of so abstract a Principle as Prana even, is the necessity for an upright life, for brotherliness towards each other; a life of purity, of morality, and of altruism.

CHAPTER IV.

FOURTH PRINCIPLE—KAMA, OR DESIRE.

THE state of consciousness which constitutes the fourth human Principle, according to the theosophical classification, is a most difficult one to understand. It will be easier to do so if we remember that consciousness is, at its base, Unity, and that all of the human Principles are but aspects, or hypostases, of this basic, or monadic, Unity. When the centers of consciousness differentiate within the Absolute, and, thus proceeding directly out of the Unknowable, start on their cycle of evolution from atom-soul to God, they arrive at a point in this Cycle of Necessity where the homogeneous, monadic consciousness, through material limitations following one upon another in a continuous descent into deeper and deeper phases of materiality, becomes embodied desire. It must be understood that all consciousness, in manifestation, is embodied—that is to say, it must not be inferred that, except in the abysses of the unmanifested, there is any general consciousness which may be classified as desire, and in which, as a common source, the passions of entities in this state of consciousness root. All thought-consciousness in the manifested universe is contained in, or manifested by, thinking entities; similarly rajasic, or desire, consciousness is likewise manifested and contained in entities to whom this aspect or differentiation of consciousness is normal. It is when entities, which start as an atom and complete their cycle of manifested existence as a god, have passed through all the lower kingdoms, have added conscious state to conscious state until they have arrived at a point where sensuous consciousness rules in them, that they are said to be in the kamic state—to be swayed and governed by Kama, the Principle, or vehicle, of Desire. For Desire must be sharply distinguished from Thought. Kama is desire—desire in all its infinitely varying aspects, as Manas is thought or ideation in all its infinite states.

The kamic state is that in which the desires, together with the passions and emotions, govern the entity; one in which there is no light thrown upon their activities by reason. In fact, there is no reason in desire; and when a human soul yields itself to the dominion of this Principle, reason is set aside, and the one so dominated becomes but an irrational, unreasoning animal.

It must not be understood from the above that Kama, or Desire, is always unreasonable and irrational in its nature; but, when pure and uncolored by any higher Principle, it does represent desire, and desire only. Yet desire, and especially compassion-desire, may be and is one of the highest and holiest attributes of Being. It is compassion-desire, arising within the bosom of the Absolute itself, we are taught, which causes the manifestation of the Universe; thus permitting, and indeed assisting, entities whose consciousness is benumbed and latent during the interminable periods of pralaya to again take up their evolutionary progress towards self-consciousness and freedom from limitation. Yet this deeper desire is not usually spoken of as kamic. Just as the Universal Life Principle is distinguished as Jiva, while that manifestation of it which has its activity upon the molecular or sensuous plane of the Universe is known as Prana, so Cosmic desire, and particularly when this passes into action, may be thought of as Fohat, while that manifestation of it which has its field of activity upon the molecular plane of the Universe is more properly known as Kama. Kama, then, as the fourth human Principle, represents all the passions and emotions of man's nature. It has its activities in anger, pride, lust, envy, greed, and a host of similar modifications. It is a Principle, or state of consciousness, which we share in common with the animals of the kingdom next below us in the scale of evolutionary becoming. In that kingdom we see its activities dominant, and almost uncolored by reason. It is true that animal desires are directed by instinct, and, therefore, are more unerring in tending to bring about certain necessary evolutionary results than the desires of man, which are just beginning to pass under the sway of reason. Instinct in the animal kingdom is the wisdom attained through the stored experience of the elemental soul of the animal in past embodiments, and corresponds accurately to intuition upon its higher plane of consciousness in man, for intuition arises out of the wisdom likewise resulting from stored experiences upon the mental plane of being. Instinct is stored up and assimilated sensuous experiences; intuition is stored up and assimilated mental experiences. From the one, the animal draws unconsciously; from the other, the man receives light, but recognizes that it comes from the very highest of the aspects of his being. For, to the elemental soul, destitute of Manas, the monadic consciousness of Buddhi, or the buddhic consciousness of its Monad, rather, assumes to it the same relation that the Higher Ego does to the lower thinking Principle in man—it stores the results of sensuous or conscious experiences in its unconscious memory. Conscious memory pertains to the self-conscious Principle, but none the less is there preserved a record, equivalent to memory, of every conscious experience of the Monad in all the kingdoms through which it passes. Such diffused and general consciousness as that of the mineral kingdom could only be preserved upon universal tablets such as Buddhi; but in the animals it is already being stored around a permanent center, thus slowly causing that differentiation and individualization which renders possible the assimilation of Manas. Such storing about or upon a permanent Buddhic center is the source of all instinct, as a similar storing about a Manasic center is that of all intuition.

Kama, then, must be studied in the animal kingdom, in order to know what this Principle is in its purity. In man it is impossible, or next to impossible, to so study it, for here Kama is always rationalized by the presence of the thinking Principle.

Kama as a human Principle necessitates and implies the presence of entities in the kamic stage of consciousness among those hierarchies which make up man's body. For it cannot be too sharply borne in mind that Kama and Manas* have nothing in common as Principles except the power of each to color, change, and react upon the other. They are as distinct as are silver and gold, which may, nevertheless, be welded into one coherent mass.

---

* "Kama" and "Manas" may be read "Desire" and "Thought," if this aids the student to a clearer comprehension.

Therefore, when we see in the animal kingdom an almost infinite number of entities, ruled by the kamic or Desire Principle, yet wholly destitute of the true Manas, or the thinking, reasoning Principle, we must recognize the fact that as Kama and Manas have nothing in common except the Absolute Consciousness in which both have their origin, there is also in man a kamic entity, synthesizing, perhaps, hosts of lower kamic entities into that wonderful, complex system of sense-organs which relate him to his material environment For, as has been pointed out, the Higher Ego of man may abandon the body and yet this retain its full vigor and vitality. But the withdrawing of this synthesizing, kamic elemental means the inevitable death of man's body, as it does that, also, of all animals. In a Universe composed of an infinite number of entities at equally infinitely varying stages of their evolutionary becoming, we must recognize centers of consciousness, or entities, preparing to pass upward into manhood, just as man himself is preparing to pass upward into godhood; so that the recognition of a kamic elemental as the Chief and ruler of the lower Quaternary in man is one warranted by, and even the inevitable outcome of, a comparison of the body and purely animal functions of man with those of the animals. Except in the all-important difference that man has a Manasic, or Thinking, Principle, he in no wise differs from his dumb brethren in the kingdom just below him. The same sense-organs which he uses to relate himself to nature they use; and, in many instances, such sense-organs in the animals are far more acutely developed than are the corresponding ones in man. Indeed, as has been often said, without his reasoning power man would be but the most helpless of animals. His body is composed of the same molecular constituents as those of the animals The very gray matter of his brain—the materialistic god—finds its counterpart in similar matter in the brains of animals, far beneath him in mental development. He is born as they are; he lives upon the same nutriment that they do; he dies, and his body decays in a precisely similar manner. No other hypothesis except this which recognizes that man is an animal, plus a living soul within his animal body, can satisfy the almost innumerable phenomena which bind him so completely and

FOURTH PRINCIPLE—KAMA, OR DESIRE.

closely to the animal forms beneath him. If there are so many conscious phenomena in man which have their plain equivalents and counterparts among the animals, there is small wonder that science, following the *ex parte*, inductive method of Aristotle, has come to the conclusion that the whole of man's conscious being is but the evolutionary perfection of these same conscious phenomena exhibited in lower evolutionary stages. That this opinion, held by scientists, is erroneous—very erroneous—can be easily shown. But such proof falls without the purview of the present subject. The fact that there are phenomena in which animals exhibit a consciousness identical with that possessed by man, and which often exceeds his in acuteness of perception, is that with which we have at present to deal. For scientists may, indeed, justly claim that, if man has a soul, then the animals also have souls, at a lower grade of evolutionary development; which assertion is true, and in strict accord with the theosophic conception of evolutionary processes. Animals have kamic, elemental souls; man also has a kamic, elemental soul, which is the chief Rector of that counterpart of the earth—his body. In the consciousness of this human elemental resides Kama. It knows no other consciousness, until Manas, the thinking soul, incarnates, and thus emanates upon it the light of reason, together with the possibilities of both the memory of past sensuous delights and the anticipation of those yet to come. Even thus illumined, this kamic elemental is still the same reasonless being it was before, but with its power for enjoying sensuous delights a thousand-fold increased, and its desire for such enjoyment a thousand times intensified.

As to the manner in which the thinking soul welds itself to and becomes tainted with Kama, thus constituting the Kama-Manasic, or brain mind, which rules in man to-day—that will be the subject for our consideration when we come to the study of the Manasic, or thinking Principle, and for the present we pass it by.

It is the intense desires of this kamic synthesizer of the human body which largely modifies the formation of the human Linga Sharira, when this is projected by the subconscious ideation of the incarnating Ego. It is again the desire to live raging in this entity, as well as desires in the hosts of lower entities whose kamic consciousness it also synthesizes, which modifies the action of the pranic lives, at work in the construction of the human frame; while it itself is at the same time vivified and ensouled, as it were, by the action of Prana in bestowing life upon the form with which it and they are thus associated. It is the synthesizing action of this kamic elemental, no doubt, which causes the formation of the Kama Rupa upon the death of the body. The long association during life with the human form causes it, after death, to again surround itself with a low form of astral matter, which assumes the shape of its late physical body. And after the human soul has withdrawn from the body at death, it still remains associated with, and its progress towards Devachan is hindered and, indeed, rendered impossible for the time being by, the clamors and demands arising in this kamic elemental. For this, as well as many, if not all elemental souls in animals, has a limited period of normal, subjective existence after the death of its body. There is no doubt that animals dream, and this ability to maintain, or experience, a dreaming consciousness proves that they, also, have the power to maintain a subjective existence, for a longer or shorter period, quite independently of their physical organisms. And in the case of one in whom the kamic desires have been dominant in its association with Manas, then this kamic elemental has become so intellectualized by this perversion of the true function of Manas that this capacity for subjective existence is very greatly prolonged; and, so long as this entity can set up vibrations upon its own plane of desire, so long will the true Ego be unable to enter the peace and tranquillity of the truly subjective state of Devachan.

It is most fortunate, perhaps, for the true Ego, or human soul, that the natural life cycle of this kamic elemental is shorter than is its own. Thus, when one lives out one's normal life, even when this is shortened by ignorance of nature's laws by at least three parts of the time it ought occupy, still old age, when this occurs at only seventy or eighty years, finds the kamic elemental with its passionate life cycle already exhausted, and ready and eager to pass into the latency of its subjective existence. This shorter objective cycle of the kamic elemental seems to be the true reason for the natural disappearance of desires, appetites, and passions, as old age approaches. But the case is far different when accident or suicide tears the human soul, together with its kamic associate, out of the body while the latter is in the very height of its sensuous desires. In this event it will clothe itself with a strong and powerful Kama Rupa; and it will be totally impossible for the soul of such an one to even approach the devachanic portals, for the clamors of Kama, the passionate vibrations of desire, will drag the ego earthward, whether it will or no. Such a soul, thus caught within the grasp of desire, and with its own will-power entirely in abeyance because it has never evolved the power of self-consciousness upon these inner planes of Being, will find itself in a most pitiable and deplorable condition; one of the most acute suffering; one which, in normal states of consciousness, is only comparable to that known as "nightmare." Just as the one who is the subject of this terrible oppression knows himself the victim of unreal terrors and vainly struggles to awaken, so will the soul of the suicide, realizing that he is dead, and yet, strange to say, that he is not dead, struggle with all the agony of his terror to return to the life which he has abandoned through his own act. A similar state of consciousness will also attend upon accidental deaths, or those occurring in war. For if the person who is killed either in war or accidentally is of a low moral character, then his condition is very similar to that of the suicide. He will likewise clothe himself with a strong Kama Rupa, and will be similarly tempted to haunt all possible sources which afford him avenues whereby to return to a vicarious sensuous existence. If, however, the person who dies an accidental death is of even average morality and goodness, then the teaching is that he will fall into a kind of a dreaming continuation of his life on earth, which will last until the normal period for the conclusion of that life is reached, after which he will pass peacefully into Devachan. For the suicide, also, Devachan becomes possible at the close of that which would have been his own normal life cycle. But the suicide has deliberately, of his own will, interfered with his own karma. He has cowardly abandoned life because the circumstances surrounding it, and which were entirely of his own creating, have seemed to contain more of evil than he was able to bear. Therefore, between the suicide and the victim of accidental death there is a wide moral chasm. The suicide must experience greater punishment because of his deliberate act; the accidentally slain, the lesser, because he has not violently and by his own free will interfered with his existence upon earth. Karmic justice thus demands only the inevitable effects following upon each cause; and if he who dies by accidental death suffers more than he would have done had he lived out his life cycle, it is because of his moral unworth, and not because of the accidental separation from his body. The motive which causes the suicide, in full possession of all his faculties, to deliberately end that which he supposes to be his existence upon earth, must always weigh heavily in the karmic balances; while he who perishes accidentally is only entitled to, and only receives, the punishment brought about by his moral unworth, and which is thus untowardly precipitated upon him.

It will at once be apparent that in these truly named "earthbound" souls is to be found the source of most of so called "spiritual phenomena." Especially will the suicide and the depraved victim of accident haunt mediumistic circles, for such circles provide them with willing victims for the vicarious gratification of their sensous desires; while such victims, in submitting to their obsession, fancy they are yielding to "angel guides" from some celestial sphere. And even after the soul has passed into Devachan and has abandoned the Kama Rupa, which now remains an astral corpse, to slowly dissipate upon the astral plane, such an astral shell may still be revivified by the magnetic force, unconsciously bestowed through the medium or the sitters, into a false imitation of the former personality. It has been pointed out that through its long association with the body, the Kama Rupa has formed numerous habits, both psychic and of a low mental order; and these, when it is thus temporarily revivified, it tends to repeat automatically, without the slightest aid from that higher mind which originated consciously these habits which the Kama Rupa repeats automatically and unconsciously. Such a shell may also be made a kind of psychic mirror, which, equally automatically, reflects the thought-images of those present, and thus gives back to the sitters facts which they already well know, but which seem strange and miraculous when coming from the lips of an apparently dead person. These reflected mental images are the source of many of the boasted "tests" of spiritualistic circles. And the automatic repeating of its own habits of thought, tricks of speech, and so on, by a shell thus temporarily galvanized into a transient but false existence, is the undoubted origin of the information sometimes apparently given by spirits of good and pure people who have passed away, and which information was not known to the sitters present. In such cases the true ego is in Devachan, and undisturbed by any of the mummery going on upon earth; but its abandoned shell, if it happen to drift into the aura of such a spiritualistic circle, may take on a false semblance of life, and repeat, quite automatically, yet still accurately, enough of the incidents of its past life to convince those present that the soul of such a one has really returned to earth. The proof that it is not the true ego lies in the fact that such communications always refer to the past; they never give new facts of their supposed spiritual habitation; they never advance any philosophical explanation of life; they add nothing to the sum of human knowledge; they are but the faded echo of former earth experiences. When spiritual communications take the form of philosophical discussion, or the descriptions of "summerland," or similar things, the source of such intelligence is again different, and will be explained when we come to deal with a higher state of consciousness than the kamic, which concerns us now.

All Kama Rupas have their local habitation in what is known as Kama Loka, and which is but a duplicate of this earth in finer astral matter—its Linga Sharira, in fact. And not only do human Kama Rupas live, pass into latency, and fade away here, but also the astral forms of the lower orders of life, and especially the Kama Rupas of all members of the animal kingdom which have reached a sufficiently intense kamic plane to clothe themselves with such forms at death. Therefore, he who, by means of a very low and dangerous kind of clairvoyance, forces his consciousness upon this the lowest of all astral planes, will find himself in contact with not only Kama Rupas and shells of dead men, but also with the counterparts of dead animals. And there is little doubt that there have been cases where such kama-rupic forms of animals have become sufficiently materialized to be visible to the non-clairvoyant eye, just as the Linga Sharira, or even the Kama Rupa of human beings, is also capable of clothing itself transiently with molecular matter, and also of becoming temporarily visible to the ordinary vision. This low clairvoyance, which seems so desirable to those who are curiosity-seekers rather than real students of the philosophy of life, is the result of resorting to practises which for a brief interval free the soul from its material vehicles. There are many such ways. Crystal-gazing and other forms of self-hypnotism are examples. And unless one has become morally pure when he separates his consciousness from his body, he will find himself upon a plane appropriate to his unclean consciousness. But if he be a pure and holy person, with altruistic desires—one whose passions are all in abeyance—he need have no fear of finding himself in Kama Loka when he abandons his material body from any cause. If, however, as is the case with the majority of mankind, passion dominates and desires rend him, he will surely land himself in this most undesirable of all conscious states and localities. He will be as nearly in "hell," perhaps, as is possible for the human soul. He will have as his companions the senseless, passionate, ghoul-like inhabitants of this horrible realm; and if he do not become himself, even while in the body, morally depraved, or mentally unsound, he is setting up attractions and creating causes which will certainly place him in this loka at death, and render his stay under such terrible associations proportionately long. For the declaration in the Bhagavad Gita, that "those who worship the dead go to the dead," or, in other words, that the attractions and beliefs which we cultivate during life guide and determine our post-mortem states or the intervals between two lives, is both true philosophically and warranted under the law of Karma. Thus, one who has longed for intercourse with the dead, who has accepted the gibberish poured out by these senseless shells as the *summum bonum* of all good that could come into his life, will most assuredly be drawn into the kama-lokic region at death; and, just as he has set up during life so many causes which bind him to this plane, his stay here will be proportionately long. On the contrary, if one has lived a truly spiritual life—meaning by spirituality the cultivation of one's highest and noblest faculties and unselfish work for the elevation of humanity and the study of the laws which obtain in spiritual matter—Kama Loka will scarcely detain him a moment. He will pass swiftly through this horrible, moral graveyard of putrefying astral corpses, and at once enter upon the peace and safety of Devachan.

CHAPTER V.

LOWER MANAS.

IN THE study of the human Principles progress is comparatively easy so long as we have to deal with the lower quaternary alone. For the four Principles—the Body, the Linga Sharira, Prana, and Kama—are all upon planes either material or sufficiently near the material to be readily analyzed, classified and understood. But when the plane of mentality is reached one of the hardest problems in human consciousness presents itself. For there are in every human breast two forces struggling for mastery—the one trying to drag an indefinable something downward, and to identify this something with itself as the "I am myself"; the other as strenuously endeavoring to elevate this same indefinable center of consciousness, and merge it with itself as an "I am myself" upon an infinitely higher plane. It is as though the human soul stood entirely apart from both of these, the lower being our animal nature, and the higher the voice of the divine Inner Ego, or our conscience, as it is ordinarily termed. And yet it is extremely difficult to disentangle the soul from its association with the lower nature upon the one hand, or from the voice of conscience upon the other. Therefore it is that we have just spoken of it as an indefinable something which yielded now to the one and again yearned toward the other. This thinking Principle in its dual aspect is recognized by theosophic philosophy as one of the human Principles in its septenary classification. We have principally to deal with the lower of its aspects in this chapter, and yet this cannot intelligently be done without a brief examination, at least, of certain phases of the higher.

Man's Higher Ego, so the Wisdom-Religion teaches, is a spiritual entity, which has attained in former world-periods an almost infinite amount of wisdom upon other worlds of the Kosmos, or, at least, under other material conditions. It now descends to this earth for the double purpose of imparting its own divine essence and nature to lower entities struggling in the bonds of matter here, and that itself may learn, if but vicariously, by incarnating in these human-animal bodies, additional wisdom through observing and being associated under the law of cause and effect with the play of passions raging upon this molecular plane of the Universe. To understand, then, the nature of the aspect with which we are dealing—Lower Manas—it is necessary to bear in mind what man would be without the incarnation of his Higher Ego, and what the effect of that incarnation has upon the animal nature. Without a Higher Ego, man would be only a talking animal; if, indeed, capable of this. As an animal, he is a bundle of instincts, passions, appetites, and desires, in no way different from the animals of the kingdom beneath him except in the longer period, and hence greater perfection, of the evolutionary processes he has experienced. The feeble intelligence observed in the lower animal is carried to a higher degree in him as an animal; but it is the same intelligence in kind. There is no exhibition of emotion, instinct, nor even of reason, in man which does not find its analogue or counterpart in the lower animals. Certain of these, as reason for instance, are only faintly seen; but others, as in many of the instincts and senses, are even more sharply developed than in man. The Higher Ego, then, descends to earth and incarnates or associates itself with the most perfect animal upon that earth, but which was before that incarnation but a perfected animal. By this association or incarnation is bestowed a portion of the essence of the Higher Ego upon or in this animal's brain. This, which before was reasonless, blazes up under the flame of the presence of the reasoning Higher Ego into a false semblance of a truly rational center of consciousness. The process seems to be almost entirely analogous to that which occurs when magnetism is bestowed upon non-magnetic iron through contact with a true magnet. The magnet has lost none of its own magnetism, and yet there appears to have emanated from it a portion of itself. Similarly, the Higher Ego, without sacrificing any of its own divine nature, bestows a portion of its own reasoning and thinking power upon the human-animal with which it is thus associated. There springs up, then, because of this emanation, an illusory entity having the feeling of "I am myself," entirely because of its borrowed glory from the Higher Ego. It is the result of the temporary fusing of this emanation of Manas with the human elemental synthesizing the human form. Without this emanation, the elemental would have no feeling of " I am I"; yet, as a center of desires, instincts, and passions, it is so powerful as to almost completely merge this ray of Manas into its own passionate nature, and to cause it to lose all memory of, or relation to, its divine source, and to identify itself almost wholly with its "body," and the desires and sensuous delights apparently connected with that body entirely, and which to it seem the sum of existence. This elemental, then, blazes up into a false semblance of a thinking, reasoning entity during the time of this association. But this can only be temporary, for the elemental itself has not evolved to the plane where this feeling is normal and permanent by many eons of years. Withdraw the emanation or ray of Manas, and its borrowed glory soon fades. It splutters and flickers for a few brief years in Kama Loka, and then enters upon its cycle of latency until again fanned into a flame by the reincarnating Higher Ego descending to earth in another body, which this same elemental, by virtue of past karmic association, must again synthesize—these successive incarnations constituting its manvantaras and pralayas.* This blazing up of an illusive "I am myself," which is not the human elemental alone, nor yet Lower Manas, is the chief mystery of human existence. For here the process of incarnation takes place. Here is the mysterious weld joining body to soul. For the ray from Manas—the emanation of its own essence—which causes the flaming up of the animal faculties in man, is capable of being withdrawn into the essence of the Higher Manas; and, indeed, its normal destiny is to be so withdrawn after each incarnation, carrying thence the fruitage or results of its experiences while in the body. It has become—this ray, or Lower Manas—an almost independent entity during its long association with the body. It has identified itself so closely with the desires and inter-

---

*Manvantaras and Pralayas—alternating periods of activity and repose. Such alternating cycles obtain in manifestation absolutely without exception ; and, being universal (although varying infinitely in their duration), must be regarded as an aspect of the Absolute, or an Absolute law.

ests of that body, it has become so colored by its association with and experiencing of the purely animal desires, so changed from its state of original purity, that it, as we have seen, no longer recognizes its source. And if it identify itself too entirely with that animal nature, then is it incapable of being withdrawn by its parent, or of returning to its source. In this case, fighting with the force of its lower will, it deliberately chooses to remain associated with the animal entity synthesizing its body; believing itself to be that entity through the loss of its discriminating power because of this association. Then, upon the death of the body, it becomes truly a "lost soul."

The complex nature of our personality is thus readily perceived. It is also perceived that that indefinable something which listens to the voices from both above and below, and which inclines now to one and again to the other, is not the true individuality or Higher Ego, but is its reflection in matter—is truly the Lower Manas of our present study. This Lower Manas, then, is an emanation from Higher Manas,[*] welded to the animal elemental within us, by incarnating in the physical body of that elemental. It remains entirely distinct from this elemental, however. The two are disparate, and the ray, or emanation, does not actually unite or fuse into its associate, as is shown by the fact that the desires of the latter are distinctly recognized as coming from a source beneath itself. There are thus two entities in every human breast, which remain for ever separate, although each reacts so intimately upon the other. But the intimacy is brought about through both these occupying the same tenement, as it were—to use a very crude simile. The better illustration might be that of the multiple tubes attached to a phonograph. The same tunes or noises are then heard by all who apply any of the different tubes to their ears. Thus, the Lower Manas receives over the telegraphic service of the nervous system the same sense-impressions from the material world that are conveyed to the human-elemental,

---

[*] Higher Ego and Higher Manas are synonyms as to the entity to which they refer, which is the true soul, but represents two aspects of that entity. "Higher Manas" accentuates the thought-creating power of the soul, or, rather, the fact that thought is an essential attribute; "Higher Ego" accentuates the "I am I," or feeling of egoity which arises in the soul— the "Ahamkara" of Eastern metaphysics.

which comes of its being incarnated in, or magnetically united to, every portion of that animal-elemental's brain and body. But, to make this simile more complete, it must be understood that the lower elemental selects and plays the tunes upon the phonograph, at first exclusively. Lower Manas is but the interested spectator and enjoyer of the performance, which thus consists in the play of the normal passions of the lower nature. But as it grows fond of these animal passions and appetites, rendered in siren music, as it associates, and by its awakened desires identifies itself with the stormy, passionate nature of the lower elemental, it soon takes upon itself the office of suggesting new delights, as well as of reveling in the memory of those which have gone, and in an acute anticipation of those which are to come. [By thus adding the light of reason, memory, and anticipation to the non-intellectualized sensuous delights of the elemental in whose body it has incarnated, it increases the intensity of these a thousand-fold, and makes the task of subduing them a thousand times more difficult. And as it thus identifies itself more and more completely with its lower companion there grows up, as the result of the association, a strange, illusionary, unreal entity, whose life is truly limited by the horizons of the cradle and the grave, and which fleeting entity is our ordinary selves.] For it is the production arising out of the intellectualization, during the period of the incarnation of Lower Manas, of the desires of that animal entity with which Lower Manas itself thus unconsciously coalesces. But the union which is so intimate during life that it is impossible to see where the one begins and the other leaves off is, nevertheless, destroyed at death. The animal-entity passes again into its old condition of a merely human-animal elemental; Higher Manas is entirely withdrawn, and the intellectualization of the lower faculties ceases. Through force of habit and through long association, the intellectual power of this human-elemental persists for some time after death; and this it is which constitutes the state or condition of consciousness called Kama Loka. But just as a dog, or horse, no matter how highly trained its faculties may be, soon relapses into its former state of wildness when no longer subjected to human influence, so does this human-elemental slowly lose the intellectualization it has gained by its life association with Lower Manas in the body. It is this separation of Lower Manas and its elemental associate that is meant when we are told that Higher Manas "withdraws its ray." The process, indeed, is unavoidable; for the physical body of the lower entity, being dead and dispersed, and that entity being able to maintain but a brief cycle of subjective mental activity, it can no longer afford a vehicle for the incarnation of the ray of Manas, and the latter of necessity withdraws to the devachanic plane of consciousness; just as the elemental of necessity passes into the condition of latency which overtakes all centers of consciousness when they fall below the plane of self-consciousness. The time required for this separation, or the withdrawing of the ray of Manas, is subject to the greatest variation. For if the lower, animal faculties have been intensely intellectualized, if the Lower Manas have leaned toward and lived in and upon these sense-gratifications, then it takes a correspondingly longer period for the animal-entity to pass into latency; and, on the contrary, if the personality has learned to control its lower associate, if the man has during life lived in his higher nature, and has taken little or no delight in the sensuous things of life, then will that elemental pass into latency almost immediately. The withdrawal of the ray of Manas in such a case is almost instantaneous, and Devachan is at once experienced. Happy is the man whose Kama Loka existence is thus brief!

It will also be seen that, if the Lower Manas entirely identifies itself with this kamic elemental, or with Kama as it is ordinarily stated, there is a possibility of its being unable to separate itself from its association with this elemental at death. Then a dreadful thing occurs; for if the normal line of union does not, or indeed cannot, yield, then must a separation upon a higher plane take place. In this case the division occurs between Higher Manas and its ray, and a "lost soul" is the result. Then the human elemental, thus intellectualized,—thus shining by the borrowed glory of the ray of Manas which it has succeeded in appropriating,—is enabled to live a brief life-cycle as an entirely independent entity. It is neither the human elemental nor the ray of Manas, but truly a compound of both of these. Having been throughout its whole life, or, it may be, throughout a series of past lives, attracted entirely earthward by these sensuous desires, which it not only failed to control but which it increased and strengthened by its own will, this "lost soul" is irresistibly attracted earthward upon the death of its body. It haunts mediums, and seeks every other possible avenue by which it can vicariously experience again the old sensuous delights. It may prolong this uncanny life for a long period; or its raging desires earthward may cause its reincarnation as a human moral monster, such as a Deeming or a Jessie Pomeroy. It will thus go on incarnating until all the borrowed light of Manas is extinguished, when it will have to pass into a condition about which it is useless to speculate. This much is evident, that, as has been pointed out, the association of personality to individuality being relatively permanent, and the same individual slowly and by almost numberless successive incarnations elevating the personality to its own divine plane of self-consciousness, the severing of this association is a most serious and dreadful event. It is an association begun, no doubt, with the very beginning of humanity upon this globe. The "Secret Doctrine" states that each Higher Ego selected its "vehicle" during the middle of the Third Race of this Round, more than eighteen millions of years ago. Since that time the association of the Higher Ego and lower personality has been uninterrupted, evidently. If, now, this association is violently broken off, the human elemental cannot go back to the condition in which it was so many millions of years since, but must remain without a hope of further progress upward, during unthinkable periods of time. For it there is no Higher Ego; and what will befall it after entering into the mysterious "eighth sphere" of the earlier teachings, it is impossible to conceive. As there can be nothing stationary in all this great Cosmos of immutable activity, and as such an entity has thrown itself outside of all possibility of progressing harmoniously under the "breath" of that Absolute Motion which is the cause of all evolution, the inference is justifiable, at least, that this Absolute Motion, which is constructive in the normal course of nature, becomes destructive in these instances, and that such entities will be slowly but inevitably forced downwards from plane to plane of the Cosmos, reversing all the work of their up-building, until they at last become practically annihilated, or reduced to a condition so near annihilation that upward progress again becomes possible. And every step in all this must be accompanied by more or less acute suffering. For all suffering is due to violation of, and opposition to, nature's laws; and this state of inharmony and opposition to nature must be the position of such an entity during the entire cycle of its almost infinite descent.

But let us cease to look upon this gloomy possibility, and turn instead to that harmonic progression of the human soul, in which Lower Manas plays so important a part. It will be seen that as we are permanently associated with our personalities, as we are utterly unable to separate ourselves from them except by the dreadful process of losing them, and thus abandoning them to a fate too dreadful to contemplate, and that as every personality represents the sum total of all preceding personalities, how important a recognition of this relation of Higher Ego to lower personality becomes in our study of human destiny! Each man upon the earth to-day is the result of an almost infinite past. His character is exactly what he himself has created. If he builds for himself a debased, wretched, vicious and wicked body in this life, he must return to a body having these same characteristics in the next, because he has never been and can not be separated from the character which he has engrafted upon his personality. The Lower Manas may, indeed, be withdrawn into its Parent and pass a cycle of comparative happiness and peace in Devachan, but upon it re-emerging from that cycle the old association must be renewed. There is no escape. We waken to life the same elementals with which we were formerly associated, and which, in a condition of latency, have been awaiting our return. We are bound to them by ties a thousand times stronger than the supposed force of gravitation which holds the earth within its orbit about the sun. So, upon the other hand, every good, moral and pure trait of character which we create in this or any life will follow us into our next as surely as the earth follows the sun through the heavens. The enemies we slay now will not return to fight us then, says the "Voice of the Silence," and a more encouraging and at the same time a more profoundly philosophical statement cannot be found in any Holy Writ. The "I am I," of each personality is an emanation from the Higher Ego of each. It is a "mind-born son" of the Higher Ego, yet the travails of its birth extend over the eons of years which go to make a manvantara. This mystery of mind-birth is exemplified each year at certain festivals in India, where, it is stated, thousands of pilgrims with unlighted torches crowd about the temple door, awaiting the appearance of the sacred fire. When it appears those nearest light their torches at its flame, and these, in turn, light those of others, and these, others, until at last every torch in all the great throng is blazing in a sea of flame, Yet the original holy flame is undimmed and undiminished. So with the mind-born. At the birth-throes of this physical race, we are told that many "received but a spark," and of these we are. With what care, then, ought we to guard this precious spark which shall one day expand into the shining flame of a perfected human soul! For "becoming one with our Higher Egos" means—can but mean—expanding and growing in spirituality until we are one in spiritual nature as we are now one in essence. So that the toils of human life do not mean the merging of the human soul into some glorious source which shall end its existence as well as its suffering, but the coming into spiritual manhood of a new spiritual being—the mind-born pilgrim of the ages!

This is the true relation which the Lower Manas, as it seems to the writer, bears to its human-animal body. Without pretending that this explanation is faultless, or that it is capable of explaining all the mysteries of life, it is submitted as a working and highly ethical hypothesis for our present environments. All finite problems must of necessity impinge upon that Infinite of which they constitute a portion. And that there are mysteries in human consciousness which no hypothesis is capable of solving, the writer freely admits. But it is claimed that this view does explain many of the mysteries of human existence; that it is in full accord with the doctrines of Karma and Reincarnation; and that it furnishes a most philosophical and wholesome basis for ethics. By it is seen, if but dimly, why and *how* that we sow in one life returns to us in our next. The relation of the individuality to the personality is shown to be not the transitory condition which the ordinary view takes of it. And, once the fact dawns upon the human mind that this association of Higher Manas with the lower personality is permanent and durable, then will the very highest incentive towards the elevation and purification of that lower nature to which we are thus united be afforded. If we must live life after life upon this earth limited by a certain and inevitable association here, and if it is in our power to make this association either pleasant or unpleasant, then is it the height of folly not to take the necessary steps; to "take up arms against a sea of troubles and by opposing end then" by subduing all the sources of our misery and unhappiness—our passionate, lower self. Recognizing this great fact, we shall engage in the battle of life with renewed hope; we shall face a future fraught with the grandest prophecies, for when we shall have united our lower nature to our Higher Divine being, if we but reach up to this Divinity, out of that union shall we then be enabled truly to pass into that Paradise where the wicked cease from troubling and the weary are at rest.

CHAPTER VI.

THE REINCARNATING EGO.

THE Reincarnating Ego, known also as the Higher Ego, Higher Manas, etc., has to be next studied. It is unnecessary to state that almost insuperable difficulties attend its attempted examination. Being at the very base of man's existence, it can not be approached by any ordinary methods of analysis, either deductive or inductive. Its origin is lost in the mists of eternal duration; and its activities upon this plane of conscious existence are clouded by the material darkness which enwraps it as with a benumbing, stifling shroud. So paralyzed are its natural functions, so concealed its true nature, that it is small wonder that almost a third of the inhabitants of the world do not suspect its existence; while of the remainder, although recognizing it philosophically, few have but the faintest conception of its real nature or attributes.

That there is an inner, or buried, ego very greatly superior to that of our ordinary, waking, conscious life is easily susceptible of scientific proofs. Chief among these stand the phenomena of hypnotism, trance, prophecy, clairvoyance, and allied states. As has been pointed out elsewhere,* the effect of hypnotism, most disastrous to the waking will, is to apparently remove layer after layer of these fleshly garments which hinder the free functioning of the soul, so that a very ordinary or even stupid person becomes profound, philosophical, possessed of deeper, and even of technical, knowledge of which he has no waking consciousness. Clairvoyance, prophetic dreams, somnambulic trance, together with thousands of phenomena whose profound bearing upon the existence and native functions of the soul have hitherto been overlooked by psychologists, afford ample evidence not only of the presence of a soul, but of the farther and most important fact that instead of aiding, widening or of almost creating it, which is the popular conception, the body limits the normal consciousness

---

*See the Author's work on Reincarnation, p. 145, *et seq*.

of this soul to a degree little suspected by even philosophic minds.

While the Higher Ego has its base in spirit, or consciousness, it itself appears to represent and to be the very essence of that condition of consciousness known as Thought. What thought is in its ultimate essence can not be self-cognized. Therefore, it must ever remain a mystery to self-conscious beings, until they shall have passed above and beyond it—a state which quite transcends our present power of conception. Viewed from the standpoint of the phenomenal universe, it appears to be the active agent in creation, for there is no fact nor phenomenon which is not plainly its result. From world to atom, from sun to man, there is absolutely nothing which is not due to its creative activity. Yet Thought requires a Thinker; it is not self-born. Unlike consciousness, its very presence is the eternal witness of differentiation; it first proclaims the dawn of another period of manifestation; it testifies to the outward flowing of the Great Breath of the Ocean of Being. Before its appearing even "Universal Mind was not, for there were no Ah-hi to contain it," declares the sublime stanzas of Dzyan. It is the universal creator; yet the conception of creation throughout the Western world must be carefully eliminated before one begins an analysis of its phenomena.

For Thought creates by entering into and becoming its creations. There is no use for extraneous matter in the sense of a potter using clay, of which he fashions a vessel entirely distinct and apart from himself, which represents the Western idea of the creative act—except that this further supposes the Creator of the Universe to first create the clay, of which he fashions his creations, out of absolutely nothing. The Occult teaching is, as said, that Thought becomes its own creations. Thus, let suppose that it is the duty of one of the Ah-hi to create a solar system, such as ours. His thought would infuse itself into and energise a vast " Body" of "primordial" matter—the latter itself already the seat of innumerable latent, or subjectively conscious, entities. With every atom of all this mass of matter the Ah-hi consciously identifies himself, just as man identifies himself with the matter of his body, and every atom thrills with the thought of the worlds to be. In this manner are impressed those primal laws, and that apparently blind purpose in nature which cause it to struggle upward along the hard and devious paths of evolution.

Let us suppose primordial matter to differentiate into "fire-mist," this into ethereal, this into astral, and this into molecular matter, and a nebula to be thus born in apparently empty space. All the future course of the newly created system is graven in the records of the physical heavens, and he who runs may read. The mechanical agent has been change in vibration, modifications in the ceaseless motion of the "Great Breath," as the Hindus so poetically term the action of "That which Is, Was, and Will Be"; but the directing, guiding force has been Thought, using as its agent "Fohat," or Cosmic will.

This is the macrocosmic process, and as its details are studied it is seen why man is said to be the microcosm, or little copy, of that macrocosm. There is within him a creative center of consciousness, associated, as was seen in our study of the body, with almost innumerable hierarchies of conscious, but—note well—not self-conscious entities. To become self-conscious is to use creative force; to guide differentiation; to furnish a center wherein the creative ray of Mahat may be focused upon a lower plane. Such a Mahatic center our Higher Egos are. As unity in essence pervades the entire manifested universe, so it becomes possible, and indeed the law, that Thought thus associating itself with entities below the Manasic plane bestows upon them a portion of its own power. In other words, it "emanates" itself, and its emanations become, in turn, "like unto their Father." This would not be possible if all things were not one in essence, and it shows that in every atom of the Universe there are all the potentialities of the highest god. That which has the potentialities of flame can be quickened into flame by the application of flame, which seems to be the compassionate law capable of reuniting and rebinding all the wayfarers and pilgrims, lost in the illusive cycle of differentiation, to their one source and origin, the Absolute. When high, creative Dhyan Choans "thought" this world into mayavic* existence, the idea of man was impressed upon its every atom, and

---

*Maya—illusion, or non-reality, in the sense of impermanency, and of concealing the reality hidden behind it.

this is, as has been shown, the true reason for all nature pointing towards and culminating in man. This primal impress is also the cause for nature's blind groping after manhood—for the creation of those "men-monsters, terrible and bad,"* which were produced by entities without the "fire" of Mind, yet still unconsciously, responding to the primal impulse which demanded "men" for this earth.

Such mindless creators could not bestow that which they did not have. They could give to man passion, emotion, the desire for sentient existence—in short, could produce an animal; but a man was an unrealizable dream to them. The oneness in essence of all that is, and, because of this oneness, the capability of bestowing their own nature upon other differentiations in the one essence, upon the one hand, and of receiving this impress, upon the other, is the key which will unlock the source of whatever of Manas or Thought man has within his being. All things are born by emanation, except the "Primordial Seven,"† who are said to "radiate" directly from the Absolute. The production of the humble unicellular animal or vegetable by fission is as truly an emanation of its own essence, upon its lowly plane, as is the creation of a thinking entity by emitting the spark of manasic fire, upon a higher. The parent which has produced another being by dividing itself is as whole and perfect as before, and a thousand brains can be set successively throbbing with thought by our Higher Egos without lessening their divinity or making them one whit less perfect than before.

This is one of the functions of the Higher Ego—to bestow its own power of thought upon those animal elementals whose outer vestments are our bodies, and thus to render them capable of starting on the long and perilous journey towards godhood. For in an eternity of endless progression, when man shall be done with matter, other entities must step into the place vacated by him, and, when their turn comes, scale the heights and sound the depths of self-conscious existence. By all the laws of correspondence and analogy, these ought to be those elemental beings most

---

*Stanzas of Dzyan, Secret Doctrine.
†Secret Doctrine.

closely associated with man, which are not the animals, as might be supposed, but those human elementals which synthesize our human-animal bodies.

And the question is an open one, at least, whether that "Ray" of Manas which incarnates in each human body is not a true division—a begetting upon the plane of mentality of another "mind born Son." If it be but a ray,—a vague and unsatisfactory explanation of its relation to the Higher Ego,—then must the human elemental become the mind-born son.

The real entity at the base of man's conscious existence is declared to be the Higher Ego. Its horizons of life are bounded by the vast eons comprised in a Maha-manvantara, with the possibility of eternal existence if it assimilate itself to Buddhi, or the Substance-Aspect of the Absolute. Standing behind the veil of mutable matter in which its various successive personalities are clothed, itself robed in imperishable cosmic substance, it knows not birth nor death; the dread gulfs which mark the boundaries of sensuous life for it do not exist. Its home is on the plane of thought; and from this divine view-point it approaches sensuous life only by the avenues its emanations cause to arise in the human-animal brain. It bestows upon the brain of the animal man in whom it incarnates its own feeling of "I-am-ness." This borrowed feeling of egohood is the "I am I" of our ordinary waking life. Its horizon of existence is bounded by the farther shores of Devachan, as the life of the human elemental is limited by those of Kama Loka. This "I am I," as we have seen, is a compound of the ray of Manas colored by the sensuous experiences of Kama.*
And yet, although its life seems thus limited, it is only self-consciously so limited. There is no doubt that the same personality attends the Higher Ego throughout all its incarnations. It is differently colored by different lines of physical heredity; but the inner entities of which the personality is composed must be the same, to a very large degree, if not wholly, else karma† would not be satisfied. Certainly, the human elemental is the same throughout all normal incarnations. It must be borne in mind that, in incarnating, it is entities with which the soul or ego is associated,

---
*Desire. †Karma—the law of cause and effect.

not abstractions. And these entities are its microcosm; constitute the "little world" upon which it is trying its 'prentice hand at governing before being assigned larger opportunities. They are its microcosm, its little cosmos; and it is as impossible for them to become dissociated from the soul to which they are karmically bound as it is for the granite mountains of this earth to suddenly rise in the air and float away to Venus; for so close is the tie which binds man to his microcosm. The rocks and mountains, the seas and oceans of this earth, are indissolubly connected with its Regent; and, although these are ensouled by an almost infinite number of lower entities, they are the vestments of his personality while he is on the earth, and cannot be discarded even upon the re-embodiment of the earth as a new planet, for we are distinctly told that the "vital principles" of a planet merely transfer themselves to a new point in space upon the death of an old, worn-out world. And what are vital Principles but the whole hosts of conscious or subconscious entities who have been clothed with the matter of the old world? Let us avoid loose reasoning, and always remember that we are dealing with consciousness, and that in all the finite Universe there is not a particle of matter which is not the clothing and expression of a conscious entity; nor no thought which is not the direct action of a thinking entity. So shall we avoid vagueness and generalities. It is far better to confess when we reach the point where our knowledge fails than to attempt to conceal our ignorance behind an array of meaningless generalities. So that the reincarnation of a world means the reincarnating of the entities which made up that world, and the reincarnating of the Higher Ego means the re-association of that ego with its old microcosm of entities. All that is new is the very outermost and coarsest molecules, made up of lives so near the material aspect of the Absolute that they can be used by almost any entity as its clothing, whether that entity be an animal, a vegetable, or even those fused into a rock.

But all this has been shown in former chapters. It is restated here to emphasize the relation which the Higher Ego bears to its humble body, and the importance of a connection which is thus karmic and almost interminable, and the character of which can only be changed by thought. The importance of this relation can not be overestimated. We can not separate ourselves from our bodies—or, rather, from the entities which compose those bodies—until we have so changed them by our thought that they become capable of taking up for themselves the struggle of self-conscious existence. Their consciousness is daily and hourly being molded by our thought, as Manas toils at his kingly, creative function among these the lower lives of our bodies. For Thought means creation,—*is* creation,—and to be a thinker is to be a creator. Above the planes of Thought we can faintly conceive of a sea of absolute consciousness, rest, and bliss; but when we descend below this there is the clamor and toil of ceaseless activity, for all the immeasurable universes are in the throes of its active, creative effort. This activity proceeds in cycles, which afford to entities a temporary respite; but it is only temporary— a brief period of comparative inactivity and rest before they again respond to the blows of the Hammer of Thor in the resounding workshops of creation.

We must recognize the Higher Ego as a kingly Creator, and these entities clothed in the material molecules of this plane as the plastic matter which, heated to redness by the flame of his presence, he is slowly forging into diviner shapes, if we would ever gain an insight into the seemingly mysterious relation between Soul and Body—between Higher Ego and lower Personality. Thought, under one of its seven modes of activity, is constantly active within us; not a moment passes that has not to some degree changed our relation to the entire Universe. The reaction of that Universe because of this change is one of the seven phases of karma.* The voice of conscience is that of our Higher Ego upon its own divine plane; for action and reaction are apparent, and it creates with knowledge of and in harmony with Universal Law. But upon the plane of Lower Manas it is not yet fully conscious, because the latter is still in the coils of Kama.† Therefore, it can only lift its voice in solemn warning when the lower self, yielding to sensuous delights, sows the wind which shall cause the reaping of the whirlwind. Happy, indeed, is the

---

*Karma—the law of cause and effect. †Kama—desire.

man in whom this kingly creation of thought is under the direct guidance of this Divine Monitor!

For the "I am I" of the ordinary man is, as we have seen, the product of the illusion of "I-am-ness" set up in the human brain as a consequence of the incarnation of the Higher Ego. It has no real existence, and fades forever, even as a seeming entity, when the last devachanic dream ceases and the Higher Ego again takes up its active creative efforts. It is well that this is so. No enlightened man would wish to carry into eternity the "I" of his earthly appetites, passions, vanities, ignorance, and selfishness. Even the Christian recognizes this, and believes that in some mysterious manner he will be "changed in the twinkling of an eye," although all nature is proclaiming by every act that such is not, never was, and never will be, her methods.

Yet this reflection of Manas, this emanation from the Divine Thinker, is of the same essence as its parent, and affords a stairway by which the latter may descend, and, still more important to us, a means whereby we may ascend to our divine parent. For its Ray, the Lower Manas, is, indeed, ourselves—our very selves, in truth,—and if kept pure and undefiled may be indrawn into the Higher Ego to share, and be, its immortality.

But such is not its ordinary fate. The thought of Manas has as yet scarcely begun to impress itself upon and to mold its associated microcosm into its own divine designs. The effect of its incarnations thus far have been, in the vast majority of men, to fan into a fiercer flame the passionate and reasonless sense-consciousness by rationalizing these lower passions which before were reasonless. Its divine labor, to spiritualize by infusing its own divine essence into every atom of the body, lies yet very largely in the future—a task to try even its kingly powers. And this spiritualization—strangest mystery of all!—we its sons have the power to hasten, retard, or even prevent entirely. By dwelling in and living for the things of the flesh alone, we can so change and color the pure emanation of Manas, which constitutes our real selves, that it becomes wholly of the earth, earthy. For Manas is pure thought; it knows naught of emotion or sense-consciousness except as these afford it food for thought. And its thought must be pure. No flash of impurity, even, can be thrown across its divine nature. For it, all the delights of impure sensuous existence are meaningless; it views them as one might the movements of a panorama of which he positively knew nothing. It knows, indeed, that they are sinful and wicked; and, if the lower self is not too debased, raises its warning voice, but no record of the act itself can be imprinted upon its own pure nature. Therefore, the Higher Ego is not—can not be—soiled with the crimes or vices of its lower reflection, although it may and does suffer because of these. But its suffering is not personal. It is the woe for others' sake, the voicing of that old plaint, "O Jerusalem, Jerusalem, how often would I have gathered ye under my wings even as a hen gathereth her chickens, and ye would not!"

Therefore, the effort is mutual on the part of the lower and Higher Selves, when the former is not too blinded by sensuous delight to attempt union with its Parent. For if the mission of the Lower Ego is to ascend, that of the Higher is equally to descend. It has to conquer self-consciousness upon this stormy plane of molecular sense life, and it can only do this by raising its passion-tossed entities to a state where they respond instantly to its creative touch. It can never know this earth until it has conquered it, and so it seems that, although the trend of material evolution appears to be, and is, so decidedly upward, this is but half the process, and is met by an equally imperious descent of the spiritual or Thought side of nature. Our Higher Egos are ascending out of matter only in the sense of overcoming it; in the struggle they are ever grasping firmer and closer holds upon it. Yet when Thought really descends into matter it dissipates its illusions, so that in conquering the world it shall dissipate its illusions and change even its very forms.

Man is thus the microcosm of the Macrocosm, and he repeats the history of his association with its matter with every new life. As the Higher Ego returns to incarnation, it molds almost instantly the matter of the Astral Round, which it conquered and made plastic to its thought during that world period, into the astral shape of its future form. This constitutes the Linga Sharira, which has been already fully described. Into it, as we have seen, the molecules of this too solid flesh flow, making man's body thus but a kind of petrified or carnified astral form. But the Thought of the Higher Ego can and does, in the case of the trained Adept consciously, and of the ordinary individual unconsciously, produce other astral forms. These have well been called Thought forms, for there is no form which is not a Thought form. Yet in their conscious production we but see another evidence of the kingly nature of the Higher Ego, and of the real hold, through it, the soul has upon Divinity. For however feebly the voice of the Higher Ego may be heard, however vague and unreal its presence may seem, yet it is present in every thinking man, constituting him one with that mighty power which brought stars and worlds into being. His body is not himself; its desires, passions, emotions, caprices, vanities, and all the puerile things which now occupy his divine but degraded thinking Principle, are not his desires, but those of beings far, far below him, and with which he is associated to conquer and lead to a higher existence. His thoughts are alone himself, and he is master of their divinely creative potencies, if he but wills it. There is no power in nature which is not his rightful heritage, if he but claims it. And the one requisite is to recognize himself as a thinking soul, hampered, restricted, and manacled by a body, instead of imagining himself a body full of false desires, false needs, and false ideals, which the equally false theologies of the West have taught him to regard as in some vague and unreal way to be possessed of a soul. And whatever his soul may be on planes above Thought, with such he has small present concern. In the Cycle of Necessity, in the onward rush of manifested life in which he now finds himself, he is a center of pure creative thought, taking an active, responsible part in fashioning not only the microcosm with which he is more closely associated, but also in molding the world which is his present home, and changing to some degree at least the very Universe in which he has his being. Recognizing this, he will guard his thoughts as a miser his gold, and will never permit himself to think a vile or wicked one after he realizes that thus he has given birth to a vile and wicked form. For the fact that all are of one essence makes it possible, and indeed almost necessary, that his thought should affect others. Under the illusion that thought is harmless, the thinker who revels in thoughts of lust, hatred, or crime, which some weaker man takes up and carries into action without knowing why, has the greater share in the real responsibility. For each thought, by the mysterious action of karma, molds his being, and carries with it the certainty of its own punishment.

We are thus gods, and the sons of God. Let us, therefore, claim our birthright and exercise our kingly function in a kingly manner. Let us endeavor to feel ourselves one with that throbbing heart of nature which is ever pressing onward to higher and nobler ends. Let us no longer exercise the divine power of thought upon the clamor of the senses; but, stilling these, hearken to the voice of our inner god; creep closer to the heart of nature, and reverentially listen. So may we find that there is meaning in the apparent chaos of existence; so may the breath from the wings of the Swan of Life fan our cheeks; so may we re-enter the Paradise we have lost, for we will have recreated it by the irresistible power of purified, holy, compassionate Thought, and will have reunited ourselves to and rebecome our own Higher Selves!

CHAPTER VII.

THE HIGHER TRIAD—ATMA, BUDDHI, MANAS.

THE study of the Higher Triad, including as it necessarily does that of the Higher Self, is also attended with much difficulty. For the higher, diviner portion of man's being, the true soul, can, as we have seen, hardly be the subject of intellectual analysis by its lower reflection incarnated in these animal bodies. The Higher Ego, also, constitutes a portion of the Triad, and must receive some attention in this relation, so that metaphysical difficulties beset us on every hand.

Perhaps it would be well to preface the subject proper by defining these differing aspects of the One Life as it appears differentiated by the differing vehicles of human consciousness. The "I am myself" of each human being is a Ray, or emanation, from Manas, or is that lower thinking Principle which is caused to appear in the human brain by the incarnation of the Higher Ego. The Higher Ego is, as we have seen, the true man. It represents a center of creative thought in the Cosmos, emanating from Mahat, or the Third Cosmic Principle in downward differentiation. Viewed as a distinct center of pure Thought, it is called the Higher Manas, the Reincarnating Ego, etc. But it has the potentiality of union with Buddhic consciousness, and if so conjoined is then known as the Spiritual Ego.* The Higher Self is Atman, and is above all differentiation, and hence is the Higher Self not only of man, but of the Universe and every entity within it. Atman is defined as "the emanating spark from the Uncreated Ray."† It belong to the Unknowable, and all speculation upon it is perhaps unprofitable. Going as deeply as we may, however, into metaphysical analysis, it seems possible to dimly conceive of consciousness which is pure and undifferentiated; which contains in itself the Knower, the thing known, and the act of knowing. All

---
*Key to Theosophy. †Secret Doctrine.

attempts to define it are futile; we but dwarf it by our conceptions. Like the Absolute, the Higher Self can only be defined by what it is not; and yet, as it must be the All, even this method fails us. This ocean of undifferentiated consciousness, before it can even approach the differentiated states of lower realms, has of necessity to have a vehicle; and this vehicle is the first metaphysical conception of differentiation within Absolute Being. At the door of life stand the dual attributes of the Absolute, Spirit and Matter, or Consciousness and its metaphysically material vehicle known as Buddhi, the Soul of the Cosmos as of man. The consciousness of Atman, thus ensouled by Buddhi, is universal, undifferentiated, divine, containing in itself all potentialities of all planes below. It is eternal and unchangeable; and, if not the Infinite or Absolute, is at least the appearance which the Absolute presents when viewed from the finite standpoint of differentiated consciousness. Therefore, being in its nature and essence eternal and unchangeable, if the Higher Ego, even, is to win its immortality, it has to do this by assimilating itself to the nature of this divine Atma-Buddhic consciousness. This consciousness of the Higher Self is One Great Whole; it can not be thought of as differentiated. It appears to be differentiated upon lower planes, as the light of a flame, seen through differently colored glasses, may appear red, blue, green, or an almost infinite variety of differing shades of color. As in the case of Atman, we identify these with the light itself, forgetting that behind them all shines the one white flame. Similarly, Atman is the source of consciousness, and, as we have said, the Higher Self, not only of man but of the Universe. How, then, is this, which appears to be an aspect of the Absolute, related to lower things? Atman is the base and origin of all the human principles; is also the base and origin of all that is within the great manifested universe, the source alike of the atom and of the human soul, of the daisy and of the sun. Herein lies the greatest mystery concerned with manifestation, over which the very highest intellects have pondered in vain, and which seems utterly incapable of explanation. In order to understand it, it would be necessary for the finite to be able to comprehend the Infinite. But, in some manner, this which is Infinite in its totality passes into infinite variation. The only possible method, as has been stated, by which Infinity can manifest finitely would seem to be for it to take on infinite variation. This variation is said by the deepest thinkers to be an illusion. It may be. When analyzed, almost everything concerned with human consciousness is found to be illusive. Yet this illusion is a very, very real one to man, and he has to patiently and carefully study it if he would thread his way through the labyrinths of this ocean of manifested life.

Atman, then, is the basis of all manifestation. It is that which sustains and upholds manifestation—that which renders it possible; and still, built not only upon, but out of this stable something is found the unstable. Yet, as there can be in the Cosmos but one Source of things, whether finite or Infinite, then out of this Infinite must come the finite. Therefore, Atman is the basis of all that is, and is the cause of all that is. It is the Eternal, Immutable Unity, underlying all possible differentiation and manifestation; and, at the same time (mystery of mysteries!) it is Itself those differentiations and manifestations. This was recognized and pointed out ages ago. Plato speaks of it when he declares that this world was formed of "the Same and the Other." Such words fall almost meaningless upon the ear, yet out of the "same" (the Absolute) the "other" (the manifested universe) must have arisen.

Compared with the Macrocosm, Atman represents, in man, the microcosm, the Unmanifested Logos, the Creative Aspect of the Causeless Cause. It is the Unmanifested Verbum, or Word. It represents the conception, to use words which are almost meaningless, within the Infinite mind of those finite phases of itself which are to be enacted upon the stage of the phenomenal Universe. For all phenomena are phases of Deity, and must be philosophically so recognized. From God the Infinite is born God the finite. The one must remain for ever untouched, unapproachable, and inconceivable—an Absolute Causeless Cause. The other is this same Infinite Mind, or Causeless Cause, exhibiting itself in the Infinite Diversity of phenomenal states of consciousness, which Infinite Diversity, as we have seen, represents the only manner in which it would seem possible for an Infinite Power to manifest itself finitely. It is the strange commingling of these two aspects of the divine in the Universe which makes Christianity, and indeed all theistic religions, so unphilosophical. Within Jehovah, for example, are blended in the most impossible and inconsistent manner both finite and infinite attributes.

But this is a digression. At any rate, Atman represents in the microcosm the Unmanifested Logos; is in man the first ripple of differentiation within the monadic Ray from the Absolute, which constitutes the base of all human souls. And just as all the phenomena of the Universe are but the finite aspects of the Infinite, so in Atman are held potentially all of the other Principles, which are, indeed, but differentiations of this, as has been pointed out. It represents the Spirit, or the father, as Buddhi does the matter, or the mother, or as Manas does the differentiated Universe, or Son. These three are as absolutely indissoluble in Man, the microcosm, as they are in the great Macrocosm, or Universe. It is only for purposes of analysis and study that they are metaphysically divided. But this division is metaphysical, and not real.

Buddhi represents the Substance Aspect of the human soul, being both the vehicle of Atma upon the one hand, and the conserver and preserver of the energies of Manas, or the thinking Principle, upon the other. It is as uncreate as is Atman, and we shall blindly err if we associate with it any of the ideas of substance or matter which we gain from contact with the material universe about us. The universe, indeed, is but embodied consciousness; and in the Cosmic Principle of Buddhi is recorded and stored the infinite wisdom resulting from infinite experiences in the past. Similarly, in the human Principle, Buddhi, is stored all the wisdom and power arising from past experiences of the thinking Principle with matter. For it would seem that, after the first and primal differentiation of the Absolute into Spirit and Matter, and the further appearance, or differentiation within these two, or from these two, of a thinking Principle, the further office of this thinking Principle was to associate itself with all the infinite states of finite consciousness, and to store the results of this experience in this material, passive, cosmic aspect, or Buddhi. How, then, has the unstable arisen out of the stable? Ordinarily, the answer from Theosophists, as well as scientists, would be, " By evolution." This is not true, if by evolution is understood the ordinary meaning given to the word. For the process is that of a great bestowing—not a pushing up of monads or centers of consciousness by some unconscious power behind or beneath them. It is a bestowing of their own essence by higher entities upon lower entities; and this constitutes the fact and the process of all so-called evolution. All consciousness within the manifested universe is the result and the product of conscious entities. Alone, Atman may be termed a sea of consciousness, as it is the very veil between differentiation and the non-differentiated. The manifested universe lies to the hither side, and in that manifested universe there is no consciousness which is not bestowed by a conscious entity, as there is no thought which is not the result of a thinking entity, and no passion which is not the expression of a passionate entity.

Man has seven principles; and, in seeking their origin, Theosophy declares that each of these principles was bestowed upon him by an entity higher than he. There is no postulating the stream as rising higher than its source. His passionate nature he gets by association with entities full of passion, out of which are constructed his body; and he, mistaking that passionate consciousness for his own, identifies himself with it. Destroy the body, and the passionate consciousness after a time ceases, although the thinking entity does not perish; showing at once the illusion of such an assertion. His thinking principle, again, is the result of the bestowing of a portion of their own thinking essence upon him by higher beings; and so on, throughout all his principles. Similarly, the earth is but the clothing of a great, divine, conscious entity, who assumes its matter as his vestments. That matter is full of countless millions of lower entities, upon every one of whom the higher entity bestows by emanation a portion of his own consciousness, and so lifts it a little in the scale of universal life. After having experienced the consciousness of the mineral kingdom, for example, for untold ages, the individualizing monads in that kingdom assimilate its consciousness, and are fitted for the reception of a higher. At the next Round there is bestowed upon them the consciousness of the vegetable kingdom, and they assume all the great wilderness of form, design, and beauty of that kingdom.

They then pass on into the animal kingdom, and finally into the human; each successive step having been due to a bestowing of its own essence by a divine progenitor. Last of all come our Higher Egos to perfected animal bodies, bestowing upon each *mind;* for the bestowing, at first diffuse and general, has at every stage of the process become more definite and specific, until it ends by the specific incarnation of each Higher Ego in a separate animal body. But in all this there is no upward pushing. The law of compassion roots at the very basis of nature; and if the ascent through matter seems a blind pushing, the descent of spirit is a divine, intelligent compassion. Our minds are so warped by materialistic teachings, have become so accustomed to its mental formula, that we unconsciously think in these channels, and so speak of a blind force pushing up life almost as ignorantly as our materialistic opponents. There can be no such thing. It is a divinely compassionate bestowing, and there is no break in this law of compassionate help, from the lowest form of life to the highest god, or Dhyani. Each receives from some entity higher than itself. As far as we can think, as wide as our imaginations can expand, the process reaches, until the mind itself reels and lets the burden fall.

Buddhic consciousness may, perhaps, be spoken of a little more definitely; although, as stated, its conception must be largely metaphysical. Man is unable to analyze it from his present standpoint because it is so greatly higher than himself. And yet this, which is at the basis of all manifestation upon the material side of nature, which is the vehicle of the Divine Atman, or Universal Consciousness, can be thought of with less effort, it seems, than can Atman. It is the soul of the universe, the physical basis of the entire Cosmos. But it must not be thought of as substance; although it is the basis of substance. It is, rather, divine consciousness, taking substantial form. It corresponds very nearly with the human brain in many of its aspects. Upon the physical molecules of the brain is written the physical history of man's entire life. There is no thought which has ever entered the mind; there is no sensation which has ever penetrated any of the avenues of the senses; no vision, however minute; no fancy, however trivial, which is not registered upon these substance cells, and which is not capable of being recalled and brought again within the consciousness at any time before the brain cells are finally destroyed. So, upon an infinitely higher plane, this which represents the material aspect of the Cosmos becomes the brain of that Cosmos. Upon its divine tablets is recorded the history of all that has ever transpired; not, perhaps, in all its minute detail, but the effects of all that has ever taken place within this Cosmos is here conserved. Buddhi, or, as it is termed in some schools, "Mulaprakriti," changes as the worlds and universes change. Just as a man may modify his brain by his thought, so this Great Oversoul of the universe is hourly modified by the thought of all differentiated entities within it, and is ever ready to respond to this eternal modification; for force cannot be annihilated, energy is ever conserved, and this which lies at the very base of all energy must give back that which it receives.

It is said that a Ray from this great sea of consciousness and substance constitutes the human monad, because it is at the base of every human soul. But this must not be taken too literally, because, as pointed out in the beginning, this is undifferentiated consciousness—is impossible of differentiation. That which seems to differentiate it, which causes it to appear as though it were separate, is the Thinking Principle; and the soul will perceive, as the lower nature is overcome, and it penetrates by its purified sight into those higher realms, the real Unity underlying all that is. It is this Unity which makes possible the emanation, or the emanating, of its own substance or essence by a higher entity upon a lower. It is this Unity which makes it possible for all men to become gods; because each man has at the base of his being that divine substance and that, if possible, still diviner consciousness; and it is in the power of each one to unite himself to this universal, eternal, monadic consciousness by maintaining a firm hold upon the truly spiritual portion of his nature, the Higher Ego, and assimilating this consciousness which stands back of and *is* himself. So shall he, if he succeeds in doing this, some time in the eons to come, firmly establish his own divine being upon these divine, immortal planes, and he will indeed find that that which is at the basis of his seemingly mortal nature is the Creator, the Preserver, and Regenerator, of this great Divine Universe. It is our own efforts in assimilating this higher consciousness which enable us to pass, step by step, higher in the process of universal becoming; and which becoming, though now it may seem to be the process of a blind "evolution," will some day be found to have been divine compassion deliberately lifting lower entities to higher planes.

But the subject, as stated, passes human comprehension. It leads us into the very abysses of metaphysical speculation, and perhaps conjecture. We can not be sure of our footsteps. Of only one thing we may be certain, and that is that as it is possible (and we can prove this every day of our lives) to lift this lower, passionate, striving, sinning, consciousness to higher planes, and thus secure as our own more divine states of consciousness in the scale of being, so it seems reasonable and logical that it is possible for us, step by step, by overcoming all that is low and passionate, to slowly but surely win our way to the land of the gods, from whence we came and to which we must return. Because the process of the human monad (to speak in terms which mean almost nothing) seems a beginning at the very lowest rung of the ladder of evolution. In some mysterious way, life from the great Fount of Life descends to the differentiated aspect of existence, and begins as a center of differentiated, but pure, consciousness. It is lifted up to a certain point by a great Manifested Hierarchy bestowing upon it their own essence; and so, step by step, it returns to the great Source from which it emanated. But in this journey, which has been termed the Cycle of Necessity, something wonderful, grand, and divinely beautiful has been accomplished. That which descended conscious from the great sea of consciousness and unreasoning bliss reascends self-conscious; and this it is the mission of all human souls to accomplish, and is the object of this journey of the Soul through the Cycle of Necessity bound upon the Wheel of Rebirth. For as near as mortal may understand the Infinite, this seems to be the object of existence—the winning of self-consciousness. Consciousness is infinite. It is at the basis of all that we can possibly conceive, and yet there seems to be an added bliss to *know* that we are conscious, to realize that we are divinely conscious beings. So that it would seem that the object of all this trouble and travail in these lower states of material environments was to hammer out of that Divine Spark which illumines all of us the spark of self-consciousness; that, having indeed descended, conscious, we will reascend with all the glories of self-consciousness, and be able to act a divinely self-conscious part in the great harmony which is rehearsed throughout nature during its inconceivable eternities. We are creating unconsciously now, but then we shall do so consciously; we shall change and modify the globe that we live upon into a divinely glorious habitation. At that time we will take a conscious part in all that creation which we now attribute to the highest gods. We, by virtue of having this Divine Ray from the Absolute at the basis of our natures, have within us this divine potentiality, because there is no force within the Cosmos which may not be raised to its divine potency; and the fact that we have these aspirations shows that they are potentialities, and that we may realize them if we will. The question is, Shall we accomplish this or not? Shall we make the fight and win for ourselves this our divine heritage or shall we go through almost countless ages of misery, and perhaps lose our souls in the end?

The way is plain. We have to control and govern the consciousness which is in our passion-tossed bodies, and when that is done we are ready to take another step higher, and so, step by step, win our way back to the immortal mansions of the gods.

CHAPTER VIII.

THE DREAMING SELF.

IN THE ordinary human life, one-third of the interval between the cradle and the grave is spent in sleep. Since, then, so large a portion of our existence upon earth is passed in this intensely subjective condition, it is well, as Du Prel points out, to carefully consider its relation to the problems of human consciousness. Sleep has been said to be the prototype and twin sister of death; yet few realize how close is the resemblance between the two states of consciousness. To the ordinary person deep sleep is simply death to all sensuous existence. It is a temporary and fleeting return to the subjective side of existence, in which the permanent part of our being roots. There is no doubt that the center of consciousness which constitutes the real base of our soul cannot be annihilated, and that it has no lapses of consciousness, even though sleep and other subjective states would seem to point to the latter fact. The apparent lapse is produced by two causes. One is the complete disconnection of the environing conditions, vibratory and otherwise, of the two states, and the consequent inability of the lower material vehicle to register and record the finer, inner, spiritual experiences; the other lies in the fact that the soul, transported rapidly from one plane of consciousness to another—or, to put it mathematically, from sensations which are conveyed to it by vibrations having a certain ratio with which it has become familiar, to those with which it is utterly unfamiliar—is unable to at once recognize, classify, and translate into terms of consciousness the new conditions and differing vibrations with which it has to deal. During the intervals of sleep the center of consciousness is, of course, not annihilated, but retires of necessity to deep interior states of which the memory, owing to vibratory changes in its vehicle, is lost long before the material plane is even approached. Therefore, sleep in its relation to apparently dreamless states will not be the principal subject of this study, but rather the dreaming planes with which almost the whole of mankind is familiar.

What is it that causes the wonderful phenomenon of sleep? Science declares that it is due to the exhaustion of nerve-centers within the brain and body. This is no doubt true as explaining one effect by another effect, but it is no answer for the real cause of sleep. Suppose that the nerve-centers do become exhausted by long-continued exercise—why should the result be unconsciousness instead of merely fatigue, as is the case when muscular fibre is wearied? Why should not rest from thought restore the equilibrium in the nerve-centers without this mysterious retiring of the consciousness to subjective planes taking place? To all these questions science offers no logical solution. Animals sleep, yet the nerve-waste of many of those which even sleep the longest— as the hibernating family—is so small that the nerve-exhaustion theory completely breaks down.

It is obvious that in the question of sleep we are dealing with a problem of cycles of existence upon objective and subjective planes of being; this law of cycles being one proceeding out of the very abysses of the unknowable, of which sleeping and waking are but examples of its immutable action. One may oppose his will for a brief period to this law of nature, but must sooner or later succumb, or else madness will ensue. Occultism declares that the *modus operandi* in the occurrence of sleep is that the life-currents become too powerful during the waking hours to be longer resisted, and that, therefore, the soul is periodically driven to seek subjective safety upon interior planes—a phenomenon whose analogies may give a faint clue to the action of the life Principle upon all planes of Cosmos, and consequently to the alternating cycles of manvantaras and pralayas, or the objective and subjective existence of universes and worlds.

Let us take as a preliminary study the lowest form of dream— that which may be classified as physiological, or dependent upon the lower brain-mind and the animal functions of the body, entirely. These, no doubt, often arise, as physiology claims, through reflex impulses transmitted to the brain, and caused by indigestion, uneasy postures, and a multitude of other similar stimuli. They may also arise out of a sort of mechanical action of the brain, which, temporarily aroused into activity in some portion of its mass, converts the slight stimulus into a kind of text upon which it builds a whole panorama of after pictures. Thus, in one instance, a drop of water falling upon the face of a sleeper, whom it seemed instantly to awaken, caused him to dream a long sequence of thunder-storm, shipwreck, etc., during the fraction of a second which elapsed between the impact of the drop and his awakening.

But the important point in even these low and sensuous dreams is nearly if not quite overlooked by the ordinary materialistic psychologist. This lies in the fact that, however absurd, illogical, or vicious even, is the dream, there is of necessity an entity who dreams that dream. The ordinary view is that such dreams are purely mechanical actions due to automatism upon the part of the brain, and that the Ego, upon awakening, perceives them as he might a picture upon the wall of his chamber, painted during his slumber. But this is an entirely erroneous view. These pictures, however distorted or unreasonable, however disconnected with each other, are the creations of an entity possessed of creative imagination, even though this be only temporarily and by reflection from a higher source. It would be just as easy for the picture to paint itself upon the wall of the chamber, upon the one hand, as it would be for the reflected picture to cast itself upon the brain, upon the other hand—which it must do, unless it be the creative act of some entity. The one is no more unreasonable than the other. Every picture seen in a dream is the creation of the will-desire of some entity or other. Since the entire absence of both conscience and reason from these low sense-dreams negatives the presence of the rational, conscience-guided soul, or Higher Ego, what is the nature of the entity whose creations they are, who perceives them, and who is delighted or horrified by them, as the case may be? Since animals dream, and since animals have synthesizing centers of consciousness, and, further, since animals in no wise differ physically from man, except that man is an animal *plus* a reasoning soul within, correspondence and analogy point plainly and definitely to the fact that a human elemental, an entity which synthesizes man's animal form as a lower one does that of the animals, is the dreaming entity and center of consciousness in these cases. All these dreams are the thoughts of that entity. No longer illumined by the manasic Ray from the Higher Ego, or the true soul having almost wholly withdrawn its influence over it, this kamic elemental thinks and imagines after its own senseless manner. Having no reasoning powers, its jumble of thoughts are not recognized as unreasonable; and, not being guided by the warning voice of conscience, or the Higher Ego, it will commit in its imagination the most silly as well as the most heinous acts or crimes, without remorse or even a recognition of their ethical bearing. Just in proportion as the dream is reasonable is the influence of the ray of Manas apparent.

That there is an entity actively thinking out these dreams the writer chanced to discover upon one occasion by actual experience. After closely observing the dreaming state for many months, it chanced that in the process of awakening at one time, for a brief instant, he stood apart and saw the working of the dreaming imagination within the recesses of his own dreaming brain. The latter was then engaged in reveling in one of these sense dreams, and he perceived, or in some indescribable manner recognized, the presence of the entity who was actively employed in thinking the thoughts which, upon the brain, appeared like pictures thrown upon the wall by means of a magic-lantern. The relation of the observer, the observed, and the thought-creations, was clear and distinct long enough for him to recognize that these idle dreams and fantasies to which he had attached little or no importance, and for which he had thought himself almost wholly irresponsible, were not a passive, drifting panorama over which there was no control from any source, but were the active thoughts and created images of an entity who, in that brief interval of time, stood disclosed as not only deliberately thinking these things, but also as doing them, for his own gratification, as certainly and as truly as the writer himself ever indulged in a "day dream" for a similar purpose. A life lesson was thus learned in a brief moment, and a light thrown upon the relation which the soul bears to its human-animal body before the "I am myself" of the writer fused in some incomprehensible manner into that of the dreaming entity and the thing dreamed, as both faded from view in awakening. For, in returning to his body from the mysterious realms of dreamland, the writer had caught, as it were, his lower self in the act of dreaming, and was enabled to intelligently view and understand the process.

Since, then, our ordinary sense-dreams are the imagination and thought-creations of a reasonless entity with whom we are karmically bound by incarnating in these human-animal bodies, it follows that by closely observing one's dreams there will be found the key to one's average mental life. For this entity is upon the animal plane, and is very far from having the power to create of its own volition the things which it dreams. It can only rummage for these among the pictures and impressions stored in the brain during the waking hours of the true man, or those in which reason is active. It must, then, faithfully reflect the mental condition of the man. The general tone of one's every-day thoughts, therefore, will reappear even in his most senseless dreams. Idle fancies, idle words, the usual things seen or perceived by any of the senses during the day—all these constitute the stock from which this lower dreaming entity draws when temporarily aroused to independent activity in the manner pointed out when speaking of the mechanical causes of dreams. The man, it is true, is not responsible for the lack of sequence and reasonless vagaries of this dreaming entity, but he is responsible, as the writer fully believes, for the substance and general tenor of that which is dreamed. Thus, a fit of unreasoning anger in a waking moment, which is dramatized at night into a murder willfully committed, is not, in the opinion of the writer, a mere added sequence of the thought in the waking state; murder was in the heart, and may have been, in our subconscious thought, actually enacted in the daytime. Or the murderous thought may have arisen into perception as a suggestion coming from this lower consciousless animal, but which the voice of conscience and of reason instantly cast out, and yet of which the lower entity retained the memory and which it carried into execution when opportunity offered in sleep. It is just these lowest thoughts, having their origin entirely in our animal nature, which are the food, so to say, of the animal within us;

and if they are absolutely prevented from arising in the mind, then such dreams will surely cease. Remember, all dreams are the result of thought. In these low dreams they are the effect of reflected thought, to be sure—of a power borrowed temporarily by this elemental from the Lower Manas, or brain mind—but they are none the less thought-creations. Therefore is it true that our dreams are really reflections of our ordinary mental states, and to change our life is to change our dreams.

More than this: By the karmic bond between our souls and our bodies, it becomes our sacred duty to humanize and rationalize, so far as the laws of evolution permit, this lower human elemental with which we are thus karmically associated. For it will return to us from life to life as the animal substratum of each succeeding personality. It is not a question of the mere temporary association of one's soul with passionate, willful, murderous, obstinate, thieving, proud, or other undesirable attributes which we find in our lower nature; the bond is of almost eternal duration. Death by no means frees us from the bundle of sins, passions, appetites, and desires which are but the normal states of the conscious entity with which we are thus associated. It plainly follows us into Kama Loka, and by its clamorings and ragings earthward prevents for a time our entrance into the rest of Devachan, as was pointed out when dealing with the Kama Rupa. It passes into its condition of latency at the close of its kamalokic stage, to re-emerge upon the physical plane clothed in a new physical body when the true thinker returns to incarnation. Thus, the warfare between our higher and lower natures goes on eternally, until one or the other gains the victory.

In this fact is to be found the explanation of the teachings in the "Voice of the Silence," that the enemies we slay in this life will not return to fight us in the next. And he who makes no effort to control this unruly animal within him, or he who allows himself to be subjugated by it, will return to earth accompanied by the same deplorable faults of personality with which he left. The fight must be made; the victory must be gained; and there is no greater mistake than that of Christians or Theosophists when they fancy that the throwing-aside at death of the lower nature, hard to control, or undesirable to be associated with, ends that association. It does not. "As a man sows so shall he reap," and as he builds in one life so he must occupy in the next; and his personality will not be a new one, however fair and innocent the babe which represents that personality may appear. Within it, as it grows older, will reappear the old traits of character, and the old contest will have to be renewed, the old sufferings again undergone, until at last the lesson is learned that the lower nature must be subdued.

The relation which dreams bear to the proofs of the existence of the soul can only be briefly hinted at. That hint has already been given in the statement that a whole sequence of thunderstorm, shipwreck, etc., was dramatized and experienced in the brief fraction of a second which occurred between the contact of the drop of water and the transmission of the sense-impression to the brain of the sleeper. The rapidity with which sense-impressions can be recorded by the brain is subject to accurate measurement as to duration. Only so many thoughts can be visualized, only so many things seen, during a given time. If the spokes of a wheel revolve too rapidly they pass into a blur. If the train moves too fast we are utterly unable to count objects, such as fence posts, along the track. In fact, our lives are measured by our states of consciousness. We can live only at such a rate. We can experience only just so rapidly. If, now, we find that the dreaming consciousness can register conscious states a million times more rapidly than can the waking consciousness, it follows that that consciousness is not responding to the same rate of vibration, is not functioning through molecular vehicles, and that, therefore, the human soul is independent of its body, and not a mere property of matter, as materialism insists. Let each one think this out for himself.

The key of the kamalokic state after death is also furnished by dreams. The condition of consciousness is, of course, not the same, but it is undoubtedly analogous. The man who dreams vague, chaotic dreams during life, who thereby gives evidence that his is but a vague, undisciplined, chaotic mind, can but expect similar chaotic dreams after death. And he will be fortunate, indeed, if they are merely chaotic. For if he has failed to subdue this animal within during life, if he has been governed by his lower nature, then his dreams will take a criminal or other horrible tendency. He will fluctuate between the commission of crime and its detection and punishment. For after death, in the kamalokic condition, we shall re-enact our old passionate life and live amid the same unhappy surroundings, just as surely as that in Devachan we shall experience and enjoy our highest ideals. And this lower condition renders this kamalokic entity peculiarly liable to be earth-bound and to haunt mediums, in order to re-experience the old sensuous delights. But this is a subject which has been dealt with elsewhere.

Passing now to a higher dreaming state, and remembering that all dreams are the result of stimuli from some source, it is evident that stimuli from the higher nature reach the dreaming consciousness as well as those from a lower, sensuous source. In this lies the explanation of dreams which have more or less signification. A high thought coming from above may not be translated with all the purity of its source; but just as the drop of water may cause a sequence of a sensuous nature, so the impulse arising from a thought coming from the diviner portion of our nature may give rise to a sequence or dream which, more or less faithfully, follows the line of that thought or impulse. The tendency, of course, is for it to become materialized and perverted, and this is why so few dreams are really reasonable and helpful. The divine Inner Ego may strive to impress some coming event upon the lower brain mind, and this may be received clearly and yet dramatized into a panorama of apparently non-sequential pictures, from which the dreamer, upon awakening, is able to gather nothing. And this brings into view the fact that it is only a kind of transitional consciousness between the waking and objective condition here and the equally waking and objective consciousness upon the plane of the Higher Ego, that can be truly classed as dream. For it must be remembered that upon its own plane the Universe is projected objectively a thousand times more clearly, perhaps, than is the molecular universe projected by the lower Ego upon this the sensuous plane. It has been said that the condition of consciousness at either pole seems like dream to the same consciousness at the other pole. Thus, our earth-life must appear as a chaotic and more or less unpleasant dream to the consciousness of our Higher Ego; while its consciousness, upon the other hand, appears to be the most unreal of dreams to our ordinary waking selves. Therefore, it is only in the fleeting moments of passing into slumber and of awakening out of it that our real dreams occur. In deep sleep there is no dream in its true sense, for then the Ego retires to its own plane of real being, and its consciousness there cannot be said to be in any sense that of dream. Happy, indeed, should we be could we unite our lower to our higher natures sufficiently to pass consciously from one state to the other, and bring back those precious experiences of the soul in so-called deep sleep, to comfort us in this illusory waking consciousness! But this can only be accomplished by the union of our higher and lower natures. It requires the entire subjugation and transmuting of our lower principles, and this conquering of the lower nature is what constitutes the Adept; and the Adept, it is said, never dreams. For they simply paralyze their bodies, and pass consciously and intelligently to that blissful, inner plane where their thoughts become actualities. And happy, if in a lower degree, is he who has so strengthened his will and so controlled his lower nature as to also be able to control his dreams, even though he be not able to fully preserve his waking consciousness upon the dreaming plane.

Thus, even out of dreams, unreal and fantastic though we may regard them, is to be learned many of the most important lessons of life. Perhaps the most important of these, aside from the necessity shown us through dreams, of thoroughly conquering and subduing our lower nature, is the avenue they afford of contacting the divinity within us. So long as we are unable, with the Adept, to paralyze the body at will, and so rise to the diviner planes of our being, so long are we dependent upon the sleeping state for our transitory returns to that blissful consciousness. And in the cultivation of the power to control dreams exists one of the first steps towards the attaining of self-consciousness upon these mysterious, subjective planes of sleep and death. We are only awake, as we have seen, at the two poles of our being; the intermediate states are truly subjective and dreaming ones. We have, in the eons of the past, attained to self-consciousness upon this sensuous, objective plane; it is evidently directly in the line of our evolution, in eons to come, to conquer self-consciousness upon these inner, astral planes, and the time for this may not be so very distant. Who has not dreamed that he was dreaming? Who has not recognized that the pictures before him were the unreal vagaries of his own creative imagination? The recognition of illusion is the first step towards its overcoming. And in the normal state of consciousness afforded us by the dreaming condition we find a safe avenue whereby to seek conscious union with our higher natures. Yogis and mediums bring about an unnatural transferring of their centers of consciousness to inner planes, through trance states induced by their own will or that of another, and all such practices are full of the gravest perils. But in dreams one may hearken to the voice of the God within him by means which nature herself has provided. Therefore, it is not the foolish waste of time our materialistic philosophy would have us believe to pay some intelligent attention to our dreaming states, and to attempt to exercise at least a moral control over dreams by the stern discipline of our lower nature, and the rigorous cultivation of our highest spiritual faculties, by a devoted attention to the "Voice of the Silence," which is that of our own conscience during the dream which we fancy is our waking life.

CHAPTER IX.

THE PROBLEMS OF HEREDITY.

HAVING pointed out at some length the complex nature of man, or the many streams which unite to form the microcosm of which he is Regent or Rector, it becomes pertinent to inquire more particularly into the relations which these differing streams, or Principles, bear to each other and to man from the view-point of heredity. To what extent is man indebted for his mental, moral, psychic, or physical traits or qualities to his parents, his general ancestry, his nation, and his race? And these inquiries may even broaden out into the relation between the soul and this molecular plane of matter—the influence which matter, *per se*, exerts; the amount of free will or choice of action which remains to the soul once it incarnates among the passionate entities of this molecular plane.

The "Secret Doctrine" points out there are three distinct hereditary streams flowing into man—a statement which even a superficial examination must verify. For the evidence of purely physical heredity, or that of parent to offspring, is plainly apparent; it is susceptible of the "proof" which materialism demands when dealing with psychic or mental problems—it may be weighed and measured. It is equally plain, though not susceptible of the same class of proof, that each soul conserves and carries forward that modification of character which is the net result of its conscious experiences. This constitutes mental heredity—the assimilated results of personal conscious experiences, which is as impossible to be carried forward in any manner except by the personal experiencer as it is for one to digest another's dinner. In any one life may be plainly seen this conscious conservation, and it is equally plain that it is carried forward life after life, and is the basis for differences in so-called "natural" capacities. The third stream of heredity is purely spiritual, or "monadic," and with it we have no present concern. It represents that necessary immutable base upon which, in common with all manifested life, the human soul must rest.

The influence of nation, or race, or that exerted by the entities ensouling the "matter" of the bodies of any particular people, is tremendous, and but little appreciated by the ordinary man. Let us suppose an extreme, yet possible, instance—that of an Adept incarnating in an Navajo, or other Indian body, in order to get into closer touch with these souls the more effectually to aid them. There is but small doubt that he would at once lose all his Adept powers—would become an Indian to all outward and inner appearance. He would be a great-hearted, compassionate Indian—one who would make a lasting impress for good upon his people; but still an Indian! And having voluntarily and consciously bound himself karmically by the ties which he must perforce set up, it might be many weary lives before he could, under the law of cause and effect, win his way back to his old state of Adeptship. So powerfully do race, nation, and country modify, that the Jews, the most exclusive and race-proud people upon the earth, perhaps, quickly respond to these influences. The German, the Polish, the French, the English Jew we all know; the number of differing types are only limited by the number of different races they dwell among. Therefore, the strongest soul must yield, to a large extent, to the influence of race and nation. In the case of the Indian, he would be shut out from booklore, for instance, and each nation would present differing limitations, which of necessity must modify his conscious experiences, and, to a degree, his character.

Let us enter upon the study of the problems of heredity with a clear conception of the fact that, like all other phenomena, they must fall under the action of the law of cause and effect; and, further, that every change in the evolutionary progress of any entity is due to thought. All heredity is due to thought—is the conservation of its energies. But not all heredity is due to the thought of the individual soul; much comes from foreign sources, and is the result of the karmic action and interaction between man, the unit, and collective humanity. To this latter class may be largely assigned purely physical heredity, for here the karmic relation the unit bears to parents, nation, and race is adjusted. The type of nation, race, and family is imposed upon the individual unit from these respective sources.

We have seen that the plastic matter of the Linga Sharira yields to the stronger impress, whether this is self-generated or comes from without. We have also seen the conflict which takes place between the different elements entering into man's nature before the final karmic adjustment is arrived at, and the soul is placed in the prison house of the body. A careful study of these differing elements will make most, if not all, the puzzling problems which confront the student plain. For with each new element there enter new hereditary influences; each element brings from its own past that conservation of its energy which is the immutable law throughout the Cosmos. And Theosophy does not segregate one factor in the Cosmos, and declare that this alone is conserved—which is the attitude of materialism towards force; but declares that consciousness as well as force falls under this law, and that the indestructibility of matter is but another mode of stating the same truth.

These differing elements, which bring over from their past that conservation of energy which is recognized as heredity, range from the divine Higher Ego, upon the one hand, to the humblest "lives" which go to build up the cells of the body, upon the other. Beginning with the lowest phase of purely physical heredity, we have to take into account the influence of the original cell, formed by the union of the sperm and ovum of the two parents, and which, according to Professor Weissmann,* "determines, alone and unaided, by means of a constant segmentation and multiplication, the correct image of the future man (or animal) in his physical, mental, and psychic characteristics." This curious and partially correct theory further supposes that such "germinal cells do not have their genesis at all in the body of the individual, but proceed directly from the ancestral germinal cell passed from father to son through long generations." It breaks hopelessly down in failing to account for the first appearance of this everlasting cell, and in ignoring the necessary fusing of two "everlasting

---
*Beitrage zur Descendenzlehre. Quoted in Secret Doctrine.

cells" at each conception—unless one accepts the Mohammedan view, that man alone is immortal while woman is not.

Without, however, digressing further, the fact remains that the multiplication by fission of this germinal cell is the method by which the entire body is built up, as far as its outward, molecular clothing is concerned. The "embryonic tissue" theory of cancer, advocated by able medical scientists, is founded upon a recognition of this genesis by fission. One can easily see the excessively minute portion of the original plasm that would be found in any one cell after millions of subdivisions, yet it is to the presence and influence of this infinitesimal element that much of physical heredity can be plainly traced.

Prominent among these is that peculiar tendency of the cells of the body to yield to certain diseases. Very few diseases are transmitted from parent to offspring in the matter of the germinal cell, and these show themselves at or even before birth. But that impress which causes the body to yield to the invasion of a microbic disease (consumption, for example), and especially at about the period of life at which the parent was affected, comes from the taint of weakness stamped upon the cells by the presence in every one of an infinitesimal portion of the germinal cell. Cancer, heart disease—in fact all those diseases which have been wrongly attributed to direct transmission—arise in this way; for it is not the disease itself which is passed over, but the tendency to yield, the inability to withstand attack, which is transmitted undoubtedly, and the only physical avenue for which is that unbroken sequence of molecular matter handed down from parents to offspring, and which is really "everlasting" in that it represents an uninterrupted physical sequence of life since humanity first clothed itself with "coats of skin" upon this planet. Through this avenue, also, are transmitted race and family traits; the dark or light skin, the Caucasian or the Negro features, and all of those physical peculiarities which seem so fixed that they can only be modified or changed by the introduction of the blood of another race. This germinal stamp, repeated generation after generation, molds the body into the general type of race and nation, and is largely concerned with such abnormalities as six fingers or toes, etc., although even here the influence of thought may often be plainly traced. It becomes of greater importance as we descend into the kingdoms below the human, and is the cause of that repetition of form and function which obtains here, and which becomes an almost absolute law in the lowest orders because mind is absent, and the entity is blindly obeying the general evolutionary impulse, or that from creative Dhyan Chohans having in charge this particular portion of the countless workshops of nature.

The moment, however, that we pass above or beyond the influence of this "everlasting" matter, we have to deal with re-embodied or reincarnated entities, or those which constitute man's microcosm. All of these are mindless, and many even senseless. Therefore, they yield to the stronger impress coming from above, whether this be racial, family, personal, or individual. Here may be classed all those qualities and traits belonging to the personality which seem to be inherited, or passed on from parent to offspring. The same passions, appetites, and desires, the same tendency to repeat similar crimes or vices which have brought the descendants of criminals into such deserved ill-repute, and which criminal taint has been clearly identified with inherited mental or physical unsoundness from parents—all these are to be plainly accounted for under the law of cause and effect governing the re-embodiment of these, (man's microcosmic) associates; and chief among which is that passionate human elemental, with its desires and appetites flaming up under the light of intellectualization. But while these lower associates seem to yield to the thought of the parents in reproducing undesirable mental traits or physical peculiarities, it is not a real yielding. The tendency to evil is in them—brought over from their own past,—and the parents only give the bent to its physical expression, or mark out the particular direction in which the muddy current shall flow for the one life. That even upon this low plane the personality inherits from its own past, is plainly proven by the innumerable instances where the same parents have given birth to both good and evil offspring.

In considering these lower qualities, as well as many of the higher, there enters an important factor in imitation. Children are adepts in this faculty, as indeed the plastic conditon of their minds makes a necessity. Many a psychic trick or mental habit which would seem at the first blush to have been surely inherited arises in imitation, and is confirmed by habit. And this plastic, imitative condition of childhood can and ought to be taken advantage of to establish habits and instill principles, if even almost mechanically, which shall aid the soul in overcoming evil tendencies it has permitted to take root in its lower associates during some past life. Herein is the necessity and the justification for the State taking charge of the education of the young, and providing wise and virtuous teachers. This is one of the many duties which collective humanity owes to each of its units.

In this struggle of the soul and its personality with its physical parents it must often happen that the latter prove the weaker, and a particularly strong personality will thus succeed in impressing its own characteristics upon the new body. This fully accounts for the continual appearance of children who resemble neither parent, as well as for that hopeless riddle of materialism—its so-called "atavism," or the skipping of direct ancestors and reverting to an older type. Reversion to an original type in the lower kingdoms, however, is but the throwing off of an artificially established peculiarity or variation, which was at its best highly unstable and outside the domain of the true evolutionary processes.

Most important of all hereditary influences, and constituting the reproach of science and the despair of materialism, are those mental traits and powers which the soul inherits from its own almost infinite past. Overwhelmingly in evidence, constituting incontrovertible proof of the existence, nature, and powers of the soul, this record, not graven in matter, and soaring above all taint of its influence, is ignored, and the appearance of the genius,—the philosopher, the poet, the inventor, and so on,—is sought to be accounted for in some unknown, unreliable, mysterious "property" of matter, which acts in defiance of the universal law of the conservation of energy; or else is attempted to be explained along mental lines by prenatal influence! The genius of Napoleon, according to these wise men of the West, arose from the fact that his mother was a camp-follower and his father a common soldier—conditions which have obtained since wars began, but which failed in all the innumerable instances except this one! Yet such philosophers would scorn the idea of this not being a law-governed Cosmos, but they must admit that this "law" acts in a very devious, uncertain manner. Genius defies the efforts of materialists to account for it by any appeal to paternal transmission, as it equally defies those of Idealists to explain it in the same way. The straits to which science is reduced is well exemplified in the admissions of Professor Proctor. He writes: *

"At present all that can be claimed is that some mental qualities and some artistic aptitudes have unquestionably in certain instances been transmitted, and that, on the whole, men of great distinction in philosophy, literature, science, and art are rather more likely than others to have among their relations (more or less remote) persons above the average in mental or artistic qualities. But it is not altogether certain that this superiority is even quite so great as it might be expected to be if hereditary transmission played no part in the matter at all." For getting on both sides of questions of which they in reality know nothing, the scientists are certainly to be commended!

There is no theory or hypothesis which will explain the differences in mental traits and qualities, to say nothing of other differences in character, between individuals (even twins) having the same parentage and other environments, except this which recognizes that the soul is a conscious, thinking entity, superior to and independent of its body (only as this is necessary to relate it to molecular or physical matter), and that it returns to earth again and again to complete its evolutionary tasks here. What these tasks are has already been shown, and the nature of the soul, the place of the weld between it and the body, fully gone into. It only remains to point out that here, in the conservation of the conscious experiences of the thinking ego, or soul, is to be found the complete solution of the vexing (without this solution) problems of heredity. It is but a shallow philosophy which fancies that a portion of the Cosmos is governed by unvarying law,

---
*Hereditary Traits.

while another portion is under the sway of mutable, chance-acting, or even of directly opposite laws or forces. All law, of whatever nature, is the result of some force—is its expression or mode of manifestation; and therefore mental force falls under the universal law of force conservation. There is no escape from this proposition, for that mental energies give rise to and are directly corollated with physical dynamics is easily susceptible of the most direct proof. Arouse emotion by thought, and, with a sufficiently delicate instrument attached to the superficies of the head, the amount of force generated may be instantly read off in units of heat. That heat, light, and electricity may be mutually transmuted into each other has long been known, and here is the evidence that mental energy uses at least similar modes of motion for its physical manifestation. Therefore, we are brought face to face with the fact that, as these other forms of energy are undoubtedly conserved, mental energy must fall under the same law and be also conserved. That it is conserved in one life is evidenced by the mental growth of the individual during that life; that it is conserved life after life is equally proven by the phenomena of genius, or of its antipodes, imbecility. For if *ex nihil nihilo fit*, it is equally certain that "nothing can not come out of something," either, which would have to be the case if idiocy were attributable to the physical parentage through heredity.

Mental energies *are* conserved, and brought over life after life, by the reincarnating of the Higher Ego and its accompanying microcosm. The most important stream of heredity, then, is that which each soul inherits from its own past. Under the law of cause and effect, which is but stating in other terms the law of the eternal conservation of energy, we reap exactly that which we have sown, and so return to earth with that character, whether lovely or unlovely, which we have created, and which is but the conservation of the conscious energies of our past. National, racial, and family heredity are but the karmic relation between us and our past, and, as has been pointed out, only direct the current of our conserved energies into appropriate channels; but have no part in the creation of those energies. Therefore, the character, the abilities—the imbecility, the mediocrity, or the genius,—which we possess we have inherited from ourselves, and from ourselves alone. No other theory can reconcile the circumstances of life which surround us with our outraged sense of justice. The babe born with a transmitted tendency to a disease which cripples and maims its mentality, which leads to insanity or imbecility, does not depend for such an evil fate upon chance, nor upon the accident of birth. The inherited disease which cuts off a young life in the glory of its highest promise has been earned in the past— is but the conservation of the energies of that past, and is not, can not be, in a law-governed, orderly Cosmos, the result of accident, of blind fate, or of the caprice of some changeful or vengeful god. Under the inviolable law of cause and effect, the soul returns with its powers crippled or expanded by its own actions alone. The race, and the parents even, are those with whom it has set up karmic ties in other lives, and it must share in the heritage of limitations of all kinds which the matter of their physical cells demands. The very forces of love or of hatred are conserved and bind the soul to the same family or persons for whom it has felt these emotions as surely as the lower forces of attraction and repulsion upon the molecular plane bind the planets in their orbits about the sun. There is no accident of birth, there is not one atom acting by chance in all this great Cosmos, but with unerring certainty each cause is bound up with its effect; the two are but aspects of the same thing, and can not be separated in reality, however much so they may seem to be by time. So that man can, under the theosophic view of heredity, set about building his future with the absolute certainty that no effort will be lost, that each step he wins upon the eternal stairway of the gods will not have to be taken again; but that he, and he alone, will inherit his past, be that past evil or good.

An Epitome of Theosophy.

Theosophy, the Wisdom-Religion, has existed from immemorial time. It offers us a theory of nature and of life which is founded upon knowledge acquired by the Sages of the past, more especially those of the East; and its higher students claim that this knowledge is not something imagined or inferred, but that it is seen and known by those who are willing to comply with the conditions. Some of its fundamental propositions are:

1.—That the spirit in man is the only real and permanent part of his being; the rest of his nature being variously compounded, and, decay being incident to all composite things, everything in man but his spirit is impermanent.

Further, that the universe being one thing and not diverse, and everything within it being connected with the whole and with every other—of which upon the upper plane, above referred to, there is a perfect knowledge—no act or thought occurs without each portion of the great whole perceiving and noting it. Hence all are inseparably bound together by the tie of Brotherhood.

2.—That below the spirit and above the intellect is a plane of consciousness in which experiences are noted, commonly called man's "spiritual nature"; this is as susceptible of culture as his body or his intellect.

3.—That this spiritual culture is only attainable as the grosser interests, passions, and demands of the flesh are subordinated to the interests, aspirations, and needs of the higher nature; and that this is a matter of both system and established law.

4.—That men thus systematically trained attain to clear insight into the immaterial, spiritual world, their interior faculties apprehending Truth as immediately and readily as physical faculties grasp the things of sense, or mental faculties those of reason; and hence that their testimony to such Truth is as trustworthy as is that of scientists or philosophers to truth in their respective fields.

5.—That in the course of this spiritual training such men acquire perception of and control over various forces in Nature unknown to others, and thus are able to perform works usually called "miraculous," though really but the result of larger knowledge of natural law.

6.—That their testimony as to super-sensuous truth, verified by their possession of such powers, challenges candid examination from every religious mind.

Turning now to the system expounded by these Sages, we find as its main points:

1.—An account of cosmogony, the past and future of this earth and other planets; the evolution of life through mineral, vegetable, animal and human forms.

2.—That the affairs of this world and its people are subject to cyclic laws, and that during any one cycle the rate or quality of progress appertaining to a different cycle is not possible.

3.—The existence of a universally diffused and highly ethereal medium, called the "Astral Light" or "Akasa," which is the repository of all past, present and future events, and which records the effects of spiritual causes and of all acts and thoughts from the direction of either spirit or matter. It may be called the Book of the Recording Angel.

4.—The origin, history, development and destiny of mankind.

Upon the subject of *Man* it teaches:

1.—That each spirit is a manifestation of the One Spirit, and thus a part of all. It passes through a series of experiences on incarnation, and is destined to ultimate re-union with the Divine.

2.—That this incarnation is not single but repeated, each individuality becoming re-embodied during numerous existences in successive races and planets, and accumulating the experiences of each incarnation towards its perfection.

3.—That between adjacent incarnations, after grosser elements are first purged away, comes a period of comparative rest and refreshment, the spirit being therein prepared for its next advent into material life.

4.—That the nature of each incarnation depends upon the merit and demerit of the previous life or lives, upon the way in which the man has lived and *thought;* and that this law is inflexible and wholly just.

5.—That "Karma"—a term signifying two things, the law of ethical causation (Whatsoever a man soweth, that shall he also reap), and the balance or excess of merit or demerit in any individual—determines also the main experiences of joy and sorrow in each incarnation, so that what men call "luck" is in reality "desert", desert acquired in past existence.

6.—That the process of evolution up to re-union with the Divine contemplates successive elevations from rank to rank of power and usefulness, the most exalted beings still in the flesh being known as Sages, Rishees, Brothers, Masters, their great function being the preservation at all times—and, when cyclic laws permit, the extension—of spiritual knowledge and influence among humanity.

7.—That when union with the Divine is effected, all the events and experiences of each incarnation are known.

As to the *process* of spiritual development it teaches:

1.—That the essence of the process lies in the securing of supremacy to the highest, the spiritual, element of man's nature.

2.—That this is attained along four lines, among others—

(*a*) The eradication of selfishness in all forms, and the cultivation of broad, generous sympathy in and effort for the good of others.

(*b*) The cultivation of the inner, spiritual man by meditation, communion with the Divine, and exercise.

(*c*) The control of fleshly appetites and desires; all lower, material interests being deliberately subordinated to the behests of the spirit.

(*d*) The careful performance of every duty belonging to one's station in life, without desire for reward, leaving results to Divine law.

3.—That while the above is incumbent on and practicable by all religiously-disposed men, a yet higher plane of spiritual attainment is conditioned upon a specific course of training, physical, intellectual and spiritual, by which the internal faculties are first aroused and then developed.

4.—That an extension of this process is reached in Adeptship, an exalted stage attained by laborious self-discipline and hardship, protracted through possibly many incarnations, and with many degrees of initiation and preferment, beyond which are yet other stages ever approaching the Divine.

As to the *rationale* of spiritual development it asserts:

1.—That the process is entirely *within* the individual himself, the motive, the effort, the result being distinctly personal.

2.—That, however personal and interior, this process is not unaided, being possible, in fact, only through close communion with the Supreme Source of all strength.

As to the *degree* of advancement in incarnations it holds:

1.—That even a mere intellectual acquaintance with Theosophic truth has great value in fitting the individual for stepping upwards in his next earth-life, as it gives an impulse in that direction.

2.—That still more is gained by a career of duty, piety and beneficence.

3.—That a still greater advance is attained by the attentive and devoted use of the means to spiritual culture heretofore stated.

It may be added that Theosophy is the only system of religion and philosophy which gives a satisfactory explanation of such problems as these:

1.—The object, use, and inhabitation of other planets than this earth.
2 —The geological cataclysms of earth; the frequent absence of intermediate types in its fauna; the occurrence of architectural and other relics of races now lost, and as to which ordinary science has nothing but vain conjecture; the nature of extinct civilizations and the causes of their extinction; the persistence of savagery and the unequal development of existing civilization; the differences, physical and internal, between the various races of men; the line of future development.
3 —The contrasts and unisons of the world's faiths, and the common foundation underlying them all.
4 —The existence of evil, of suffering, and of sorrow—a hopeless puzzle to the mere philanthropist or theologian.
5.—The inequalities in social condition and privilege; the sharp contrasts between wealth and poverty, intelligence and stupidity, culture and ignorance, virtue and vileness; the appearance of men of genius in families destitute of it, as well as other facts in conflict with the law of heredity; the frequent cases of unfitness of environment around individuals, so sore as to embitter disposition, hamper aspiration and paralyze endeavor; the violent antithesis between character and condition; the occurrence of accident, misfortune, and untimely death—all of them problems solvable only by either the conventional theory of Divine caprice or the Theosophic doctrines of Karma and Reincarnation.
6 —The possession by individuals of psychic powers—clairvoyance, clairaudience, etc., as well as the phenomena of psychometry and statuvolism.
7.—The true nature of genuine phenomena in spiritualism, and the proper antidote to superstition and to exaggerated expectation.
8.—The failure of conventional religions to greatly extend their areas, reform abuses, reorganize society, expand the idea of brotherhood, abate discontent, diminish crime, and elevate humanity, and an apparent inadequacy to realize in individual lives the ideal they professedly uphold.

As to the extension of its philosophy, it offers:

1.—That of intellectual inquiry—to be met by works in Public Libraries, etc.
2.—That of desire for personal culture—to be met partly by the books prepared for that specific end, partly by the periodical Magazines expounding Theosophy.
3.—That of personal identification with the Theosophical Society, an association formed in 1875 with three aims—to be the nucleus of a Universal Brotherhood; to promote the study of Aryan and other Eastern literatures, religions and sciences; to investigate unexplained laws of nature and the psychical powers latent in man. Adhesion to the first only is a prerequisite to membership, the others being optional. The Society represents no particular creed, is entirely unsectarian, and includes professors of all faiths, only exacting from each member that toleration of the beliefs of others which he desires them to exhibit towards his own

Membership in the Theosophical Society may be either "at large" or in a local Branch. Applications for membership in a Branch should be addressed to the local President or Secretary; those "at large" to any Branch President or to the General Secretary, Wm. Q. Judge, 144 Madison Ave., New York, and the latter should inclose $2.00 for entrance fee and 50 cents for diploma, and $1.00 yearly dues. Information as to organization and other points may also be obtained from Secretary Pacific Coast Corporation, Mercantile Library Building, San Francisco.

There are now, 1895, one hundred Branches in the United States, including all the principal cities, among which may be noted New York, Philadelphia, Chicago, St. Louis, San Francisco, Los Angeles, Minneapolis, Washington, Cincinnati, Boston, Omaha, San Diego, Denver, Salt Lake, New Orleans, etc.

The Pacific Coast Committee,
530 Golden Gate Ave., San Francisco, Ca

Adventure among the Rosicrucians, paper, 50c; cloth	$ .75
Animal Magnetism—Binet and Fere	1.50
Astral Light—Nizida	.75
Atlantis—Donnelly	2.00
Bhagavad-Gita—Judge, red leather, 75c; morrocco	1.00
Bhagavad-Gita Mohini's translation and notes	2.00
Bœhme, Jacob, Life and Doctrines of	2.50
Buddha, Life of—Lillie	2.25
Buddha, Life of the—Rockhill	3.00
Buddhist Catechism—Olcott	.40
Buried Alive—Hartman........cloth	.75
Christos—Buck	.60
Clothed with the Sun, paper, 50; cloth	1.25
Coming Race—Lytton............paper	.10
Compendium, Raja-Yoga Philosophy	1.25
Death and After?—Besant	.35
Discourses on the Bhagavad-Gita	.75
Dreams and Dream-Stories—Kingsford, paper, 50c; cloth	1.25
Dreams of the Dead—Stanton, paper, 50c; cloth	1.00
Echoes from the Orient—Judge	.50
Elixir of Life—By a Chela........paper	.15
Esoteric Buddhism—Sinnett, paper, 50c; cloth	1.25
Esoteric Basis of Christianity, part 1	.10
" " " " part 2	.10
Evolution according to Theosophy	.10
Five Years of Theosophy..........cloth	3.25
From the Caves and Jungles of Hindustan—Blavatsky	2.50
Gems from the East—Blavatsky	1.00
Geomancy, Principles of Astrological	1.25
Geometric Psychology—Betts and Cook	2.50
Glossary, Theosophical—H. P. B.	3.50
Golden Stairs, Tales from the Wonder World—Waite	.75
Guide to Theosophy (printed in India)	1.50
Hints on Esoteric Theosophy and Idyll of White Lotus......paper, 50c; cloth	1.25
Idea of Ne. Birth—Arundale	1.25
Imitation of Buddha, The	1.00
Incidents in Life of Mme. Blavatsky	3.00
Indianapolis Letters on Theosophy	.10
In the Pronaos of the Temple of Wisdom—Hartman	2.00
Isis Unveiled—Blavatsky	7.50
Jehosua, Life of—Hartmann	1.50
Kabbalah Unveiled—Mather	3.00
Karma—Sinnett ....cloth	.75
Key to Theosophy—Blavatsky	1.50
Letters That Have Helped Me	.50
Light of Asia........paper, 25c; cloth	1.00
Light on the Path—M. C... ...vellum	.35
" " with comments from *Lucifer*, pocket edition........cloth	.40
same, with comments..........paper	.25
Magic, White and Black—Hartmann, paper 50c; cloth	1.25
Man, Fragments on Forgotten History	1.25
Memorial Articles of H. P. Blavatsky	.35
Modern Theosophy—Wright. paper, 50c; cloth	1.00
My Books—H. P. B.	.
Mysteries of Magic—Eliphas Levi	3.
Mystic Quest—Kingsland	1.
Nature and aim of Theosophy—Buck	.
Nature's Finer Forces—Rama Prasad	1.
Neila Sen..........paper 50c; cloth	1.
Nightmare Tales............paper	.
Ocean of Theosophy, paper 50c; cloth	1.
Occult Science in Medicine—Hartmann	1.
Occult Sciences The—Waite	2.
Occult World—Sinnett, paper, 50c: cloth	1.
Patanjali's Yoga Aphorisms—Am. ed., red leather, 75c.; morocco	1.
Pearls of Faith—Edwin Arnold	1.
Perfect Way ....paper 50c; cloth	1.
Perfect Way in Diet—Kingsford	.
Philosophy of Mysticism ....2 vols.	7.
Posthumous Humanity—D Assier	2.
Problems of the Hidden Life—Pilgrim	1.
Psychometry and Thought Transference ....paper,	.
Purpose of Theosophy—Mrs. Sinnett paper 15c; cloth	.
Rationale of Mesmerism—Sinnett	1.
Reincarnation—Anderson, paper 50c; cloth	1.
Reincarnation—Besant	.
Reminiscences of H. P. B. and the *Secret Doctrine*—Countess Wachtmeister, paper, 50c; cloth	.
Rosicrucians, History of the—Waite	2.
Sankhya Karika (with commentary)	1.
Secret Doctrine—Blavatsky	12.
Secret of Death—Edwin Arnold	1.
Secret Symbols of the Rosicrucians	6.
Seven Principles of Man—Besant	.
Simon Magus........paper, 1.75; cloth	2.
Song Celestial—Bhagavad Gita, verse	1.
Songs of the Lotus Circle	.
Soul of Things—Denton..........3 vols.	4.
Sound and Music—Nahm	3.
Source of Measures—Skinner	5.
Strange Story, A—Lytton........paper	.
Study of Man—Buck	2.
Theosophy or Psychological Religion	3.
Theosophy, Religion, Occult Science	2.
Theosophy and its Evidences—Besant	.
Things Common to Christianity and Theosophy	.
Three Sevens—Phelons	1.
Through the Gates of Gold—M. C.	.
Topics in Karma—Fullerton	.
Topics in Reincarnation—Fullerton	.
Transactions Blavatsky Lodge, No. 1	.
" " " No. 2	.
Unknown Life of Jesus Christ	1.
Voice of the Silence—Blavatsky, red leather 75c; morrocco	1.
Wilkesbarre Letters on Theosophy	.
Wonder Light and Other Tales for Children—Ver Planck	.
Working Glossary for Theosophical Students	.
Yoga Sutra of Patanjali ....boards	1.
Zanoni—Lytton ....paper	.

LIST OF THEOSOPHICAL PUBLICATIONS.

The Path.
A Magazine devoted to the Brotherhood of Humanity, Theosophy in America, and the Study of Occult Science, Philosophy and Aryan Literature. Edited by William Q. Judge. A special feature of *The Path* consists in articles giving the experiences of students in Occultism. Subscriptions, 8s. per annum, post free. New York: 144 Madison Avenue.

The Irish Theosophist.
The third volume began October, 1894, and contains articles by Jasper Niemand, William Q. Judge, Mrs. Annie Besant, Che-Yew-Tsang and others. Publishing office, 3 Upper Ely Place, Dublin, Ireland. Subscriptions may be sent to the PATH. Price, $1.00 per year. Members of the T. S. will soon find it indispensable.

Echoes from the Orient.
A broad outline of Theosophical Doctrines. By William Q. Judge. Attractively bound in light cloth with colored side-stamp. 50 cents.

The Bhagavad Gita.
Fifth American Edition, revised by William Q. Judge. Printed on wood-cut paper, bound in flexible morocco with gilt edges and round corners, $1 00. Flexible red leather, round corners and red edges, 75 cents.

Letters that have Helped Me.
Compiled by Jasper Niemand. Printed on handsome super-calendered paper, same size page as the *Ocean of Theosophy*. Light cloth with olive-green side stamp. 50 cents.

Patanjali's Yoga Aphorisms.
An interpretation by William Q. Judge. Printed on wood-cut paper, uniform in size with *Bhagavad-Gita*.. In flexible morocco, gilt edges and round corners, $1.00. Flexible red leather, round corners and red edges, 75 cents.

The Voice of the Silence.
A new edition from new plates, on wood-cut paper, uniform in size with *Bhagavad-Gita* and *Patanjali's Yoga Aphorisms*. In this edition the notes are printed on the page with the text to which reference is made. It also includes the *Stanzas of Dzyan*, on which the *Secret Doctrine* is based, and contains a fine half-tone portrait of H. P. Blavatsky. In flexible morocco round corners and gilt edges, $1.00. Flexible red leather, round corners and red edges, 75 cents.

Twelve Principal Upanishads.
Translated into English with notes from the COMMENTARIES of SANKARACHARYA and the GLOSS of ANANDAGIRI. 710 pages, cloth, $3.00

Occult Science in Medicine.
By Franz Hartmann, M. D. Contents: Introduction. Chapter I, The Constitution of Man; Chapter II, The Four Pillars of Medicine; Chapter III, The Five Causes of Disease; Chapter IV, The Five Classes of Physicians; Chapter V, The Medicine of the Future. Cloth, $1.25.

Photographs of W. Q. Judge.
By Sarony, of New York. Cabinet, 50 cents. Cabinet, (bromide) 75 cents. Life-size, (bromide) $6.00. Sent by mail or express, charges paid, on receipt of price. All orders to be sent to Dr. T. P. Hyatt, 147 Hancock Street, Brooklyn, N. Y.

A Study of Man
And the way to Health. By J. D. Buck, M. D. Contains chapters on Matter and Force, The Phenomenal World, Life, Polarity, Living Forms, Planes of Life, The Nervous System, Consciousness, Health and Disease, Sanity and Insanity, Involution and Evolution of Man, etc. pp. xxii, and 302. Half Russia $2.50.

Nature's Finer Forces.
The Science of Breath and PHILOSOPHY of the TATTVAS. By Rama Prasad, M. A. Contents: The Tattvas; Evolution; The Mutual Relation of the Tattvas and of the Principles; Prana; The Mind; The Cosmic Picture Gallery; The Manifestations of Psychic Force; Yoga---The Soul; The Spirit; The Science of Breath; Glossary. Second and revised edition Cloth, $1.50.

An Outline of the Principles
of MODERN THEOSOPHY. By Claude Falls Wright. With an introduction by William Q. Judge. pp. ix and 188. Chapter I, The Arcane Philosophy; Chapter II, Cosmological; Chapter III, The Planetary World; Chapter IV, Anthropological; Chapter V, Masters of Wisdom; Chapter VI, The Theosophical Society; Chapter VII, Conclusion. Appendix I, Theosophy and Modern Science. Appendix II, Bibliography of Theosophy. Paper, 50 cents; Cloth, $1.00.

Things Common to
CHRISTIANITY and THEOSOPHY. Papers read before the Aryan T. S., New York, Jan. 9th, 1894, by Alexander Fullerton, H. S. Budd, J. H. Fussell, Leon Landsberg, and William Q. Judge. Price 10 cents.

The Philosophy of Mysticism.
By Carl Du Prel, Dr. Phil. Translated from the German by C. C. Massey. Two volumes, octavo, cloth, $7.50.

The Source of Measures.
Key to the Hebrew-Egyptian Mystery. By J. Ralston Skinner. Second edition with supplement. Octavo, cloth, $5 00.

Songs of the Lotus Circle.
With Music. Arranged by Tregina. Foolscap, bound in limp linen cloth, 50 cents.

Driftings in Dreamland,
Poems, by Jerome A. Anderson. Neatly bound in cloth, $1.00. Address the author, 1170 Market Street, San Francisco.

In its Relation to Re-Birth, Evolution, Post-Mortem States, the Compound Nature of Man, Hypnotism, Etc.

BY JEROME A. ANDERSON, M. D., F. T. S.

CONTENTS.

INTRODUCTION. The Nature and Origin of the Soul.—The three Absolute Hypostases—Consciousness, Substance, Force. ...*CHAPTER I.—The Physiological Evidence of the Existence of the Soul.*—No Physiological Basis for the Unity of Consciousness—Memory—Feeling, Etc.—Mechanical Motion Cannot Originate Sensation .. *II.--The Psychological Evidence of the Existence of the Soul.*—The Nature of Dream—Trance—Clairvoyance—Thought Transference, Etc .. *III.—The Evolution of the Soul.*—The Unit of Consciousness—from Atom to God by the Widening of the Conscious Area Through Experience, Etc....*IV.—The Individualization of the Soul.*—Centers of Consciousness Freed by Pralayas—The Cycle of Necessity ...*V.—Reincarnation—Philosophic and Logical Evidence.*—Failure of One Birth Theories—Life only to be Explained Philosophically by Reincarnation....*VI.—Reincarnation—The Scientific Evidence.*—Bulbs—Seeds—Metamorphosis of Insects—Genius—Idiocy—Prodigies, Etc....*VII.—The Composite Nature of the Soul.*—The Seven Aspects of the One Center of Consciousness ...*VIII.—The Reincarnating Ego.*—The Nature and Functions of the Higher Ego ...*IX.—The Personality.*—The Animal Man—How Related to the Divine Man....*X.—Post-Mortem States of Consciousness.*—Devachan—Kama Loca and Nirvana—Nature of... *XI.—Hypnotism and the Human Soul.*—Hypnotic Processes and States of Consciousness....*XII.—Objections to Reincarnation.*—Loss of Memory Explained—Other Objections Answered.. *XIII.—Karma.*—The law of Cause and Effect on all Planes .. *XIV.—Ethical Conclusions...APPENDIX A.—Reincarnation as Applied to the Sex Problem...APPENDIX B. Embryology and Reincarnation.—The Nutrition of the Fetus.*

—THE—
✺OCEAN OF THEOSOPHY✺
—BY—
WM. Q. JUDGE, F. T. S.

This work is designed to give the general reader some knowledge of the most important Theosophical Doctrines, and at the same time it will be of great value to students in the Theosophical Society. It contains 17 chapters and gives a clear idea of the fundamental principles of the Wisdom-Religion. The following is a brief synopsis of the book:

Chapter I deals with the general aspects of Theosophy, and that ever-interesting subject, the MASTERS ...Chap. II—Is a concise presentation of Evolution and its records in ancient chronologies....Chap. III—Deals with our Earth more particularly—shows its septenary nature, and its relation to other planets of our plane. ..Chap. IV—Applies this septenary division to man, and deals with his "Principles" in a general way. ..Chap. V—Takes up the Body and Astral Body....Chap. VI—Examines the nature of Kama....Chap. VII—Of Manas, or the Thinking Principle; all together, forming, perhaps, the clearest explanation yet written of the nature and functions of these Principles....Chaps. VIII, IX and X deal with Reincarnation and its evidences....Chap. XI—With Karma....Chaps. XII and XIII—With Post-Mortem Existence....Chap. XIV—With Cycles.... Chap. XV—With the Derivation of Man, the Apes, etc....Chaps. XVI and XVII—With Psychic Force, "Spiritualism," and allied topics.

Cloth, $1.00 ; paper, 50c.

Mailed, post-paid, on receipt of price.

THE PATH,
144 Madison Avenue, New York.

Or, THE P. C. COMMITTEE, 530 Golden Gate Avenue, Mercantile Library Building.

The above work, containing 250 pages, handsomely bound, sent post paid on receipt of price:

Cloth, (Blue and Gold,)...$1.00.
Same in Paper Covers,..,....... .50.

Address the Author,   JEROME A. ANDERSON, M. D.,
                                     1170 Market St., San Francisco, California.